SEX,
SORCERY,
_A_N_D SPIRIT

SEX, SORCERY, AND SPIRIT

THE SECRETS OF EROTIC MAGIC

JASON MILLER

(INOMINANDUM) author of *Protection & Reversal Magick*

New Page Books
A division of The Career Press, Inc.
Pompton Plains, N.J.

SEX, SORCERY, AND SPIRIT
EDITED AND TYPESET BY KARA KUMPEL
Cover design by the Book Designers
Interior illustrations by Matthew Brownlee
Printed in the U.S.A.

To order this title, please call toll-free 1-800-CAREER-1 (NJ and Canada: 201-848-0310) to order using VISA or MasterCard, or for further information on books from Career Press.

The Career Press, Inc.
220 West Parkway, Unit 12
Pompton Plains, NJ 07444
www.careerpress.com
www.newpagebooks.com

Library of Congress Cataloging-in-Publication Data
Miller, Jason, 1972-
  Sex, sorcery, and spirit : the secrets of erotic magic / by Jason Miller.
    pages cm
  Includes bibliographical references and index.
  ISBN 978-1-60163-332-3 (alk. paper) -- ISBN 978-1-60163-452-8 (ebook : alk. paper) 1. Sex--Miscellanea. 2. Magic. 3. Sex--Religious aspects. I. Title.

BF1623.S4M55 2014
133.4'3--dc23

2014036115

Acknowledgments

First and foremost I wish to thank my wife and children for their patience and encouragement during the writing of this book. They are the inspiration for all that I do.

Special thanks to Matthew Brownlee for more than 20 years of friendship and for providing all the artwork in this book. Bang-up job my friend, as always.

Thanks to Lama Vajranatha (John Myrdhin Reynolds) for providing access to countless private translations and personal teachings on tantra and Dzogchen. Also for roping me in to the Ordo Templi Orientis (OTO) *and* The Nyingma Orders. I have no idea what I would be if I had not met you when I was still a know-it-all teenager.

Thanks to Christopher Bradford of the Ordo Octopi Nigiri Pulveri for providing access and permission to quote order documents. Also for constant feedback as I wrote the chapters.

Thanks to Cliff and Micha Pollick for initiation into the Chthonic Auranian Temple and for many teachings on Sex Magic and thoughts on the radical Freedom Inherent in Thelema.

Thanks to my apprentices for sharing experiences and offering up questions that I hopefully answered in the text. Special nods to Stephanie Austin and Myles McPherson for questions on the chapters. Thanks to my students and readers, without whom I would not be able to live this wonderful life I am living.

Thanks to Michael Strojan and Jade Yu for answering questions and providing references for LGBT issues.

Thanks to all my initiators, mentors, teachers, friends, and informants who have revealed to me the secrets of their craft. Special thanks for this go to: John Myrdhin Reynolds, Namkhai Norbu, Lopon Tenzin Namdak, Kunzang Dorje Rinpoche, Cliff and Misha Pollick, catherine yronwode, +Shawn Knight, Tau Nemesius, Paul Hume, Simon, Lama Wangdor, Blanch Krubner, Dr. Jim, and all my brothers in the Terra Sancta Sodality.

Lastly I want to thank all at New Page Press who worked on this book. Specifically Laurie Kelly-Pye who read an article of mine on witchvox.com and suggested I start writing books.

Contents

Introduction   9

CHAPTER 1: A Story from the East and a
            Story from the West   15

CHAPTER 2: The Perils of Passion:
            The Dangers of Sexual Sorcery   23

CHAPTER 3: The Subtle Body Laid Bare:
            Channels, Centers, and Drops   35

CHAPTER 4: The Dragon's Breath:
            Breathing Techniques and the
            Inner Fire Practice   53

CHAPTER 5: Flying Solo:
The Sorcery of Celibacy
and Masturbation   71

CHAPTER 6: When Gods Get it On:
Invocation, God-Forms, and Sex   85

CHAPTER 7: Energy, Ecstasy, and Enchantment:
Working with Sex, Fire, and Mind   105

CHAPTER 8: The Elixir of Life:
The Sorcery of Sexual Fluids   119

CHAPTER 9: It's Alive!
Homunculi and Artificial Spirits   137

CHAPTER 10: Raise Your Spirits:
Sex for and with Angels, Demons,
Gods, and Spirits   151

CHAPTER 11: A Different Kind of Spellbinding:
The Sorcery of BDSM   169

Appendix: 4 Rites of Sexual Sorcery   183

Notes   197

References and Resources   205

Index   209

About the Author   217

Introduction

The role of sex and passion in spirituality has been an uneasy one. Sex is one of the most primal drives for the human animal, and it is the gateway to life's greatest ecstasies as well as its deepest pains and poisons. So powerful is this drive that most spiritual paths attempt to marginalize, bind, or vilify it as a force that is at best a distraction from a spiritual life and at worst a force of evil and bondage. There has, however, been a small minority of cults and individuals operating at the margins of every religion and culture on earth that seeks to harness the potency of these passions. Through special sexual techniques, passion becomes the fuel for both spiritual realization and practical sorcery.

When it comes to teachers I have always been lucky. Very early in my occult career I made contact with individuals from both Eastern and Western traditions who were kind enough to offer me personal instruction, including teachings on sex.

I learned about sex magic when I was still a teenager working my way through Donald Michael Kraig's classic *Modern Magick*. After doing some promising experiments from that book I decided to look closer at Sex Magic and started, as many do, with the teachings of Aleister Crowley. Eventually I joined the Ordo Templi Orientis (OTO), a group that upholds Crowley's philosophy and practices Sex Magic at it higher degrees. Unsatisfied with the rate of progress offered to aspirants in the OTO, I eventually left to join an off-shoot: The Chthonic Auranian Temple, where I was able to receive direct instruction and a more open access to the necessary materials thanks to my initiators, Cliff and Micha Pollick.

Eventually my sights turned eastward and I started studying Himalayan Tantra. Though I have had many teachings and initiations from Lamas of all the major Tibetan traditions, as well as Bon, the indigenous religion of Tibet, it was under the direction of Lama Vajranatha (John Myrdhin Reynolds) that my understanding of sexual yoga came together and was put into context. Without his direction, I would not have been able to understand the fundamentals, and I would not have gotten other Lamas who ordinarily are very silent on the subject to speak freely and frankly about what is really needed and important.

Throughout the last decade or so my teachings from the East and the West have intermingled in my mind, each informing the other, and giving rise to a cohesive teaching that has proven itself both workable and effective. Unfortunately in both the East and the West, the teachings on sexual magic have been shrouded by dire oaths of secrecy, twilight language, alchemical codes, and in some cases long and unnecessary preliminaries that have more to do with keeping young monks occupied all day than they do with actually being necessary for training. I believe that the time has come for this to change. The time has come to speak of these things openly and plainly.

To be clear, this is not a book about sacred sexuality: although you certainly need to hold sexuality sacred in order to make magic, the work of this book goes far beyond merely treating sex as a sacramental act. This is not a love manual either: although the reader may gain some tips for performance, the focus on the book is on sorcery and spiritual ascent, not on improved orgasms or recapturing lost libido. Finally, it is not a book of spells to find sex partners: although such Sorcery has its place, that is not what we are dealing with here. The book you hold in your hand is a manual of sexual sorcery: the art of using sex acts to cause changes in consciousness and the world around us.

I am going to present these methods in as clear and easy to understand a manner as I can. I will be speaking as freely and frankly about the topic as my teachers have to me. Moreover, I will be actively encouraging you to put these teachings into practice.

Dealing with Objections

This book is bound to upset some people. Some will object that I am teaching techniques that should only be taught within the context of their culture and religion of origin. Others will claim that any sex sorcery or yogas are dangerous unless one has spent years in training. Still others will be upset that I am tossing together "spiritual" methods with "sorcery" and thus polluting something sacred and holy with materialistic concerns. Yet others will object to the material as needlessly shocking or immoral.

To those who are worried about the evils of cultural appropriation I say that I in no way am claiming to represent a traditional path. Though I certainly borrow techniques from traditions like tantra, Taoism, and ceremonial magic, I am not claiming to represent any religion or order; no one can own a way of breathing, a way of concentrating, or a way of having sex. Like a botanist who finds a traditional medicine from a shaman in the Amazon and then applies it to a larger world, I am knowingly presenting some old things in a new way for a new audience. I do it because these things work. They work regardless of culture or religion; they just work.

To those who are concerned about the dangers of sex sorcery, I agree that there are very real dangers. I devote an entire chapter to it later in the book. This does not mean that those dangers should deter us from practice. Many of the dangers cited 100 years ago are based on puritanical Victorian ideals that we find laughable today.

To those who feel that sex magic is somehow shocking or provides an excuse for "immoral acts," I would point out that the world we live in today is not the world of 100 years ago. People today are having sex outside of marriage—this is the norm. Gay, lesbian, transsexual, and bisexual people are able to express their love with increasing openness, freedom, and acceptance. Books that would make the Marquis De Sade blush are now *New York Times* best-sellers, and the Internet serves up a cornucopia of images and movies that show every conceivable type of sex act. It seems silly that the idea of Sex Magic would be so shocking that ladies would collapse with the vapors at the merest mention of it.

Finally, to those who are concerned that I am sullying spiritual practices meant to lead to enlightenment with materialistic practices such as spell-casting and sorcery, all I can say is that I view them as being linked pursuits. Without spiritual advancement, power is shortsighted. Without power, spiritual advancement is lame. In the West we sometimes have a whitewashed idea of Buddhism and Taoist practices, but the Tantras and Taoist tradition are filled with spells and magic aimed at everything from promoting health to destroying enemies to winning the love of young ladies.

I hope that by presenting the methods of sexual sorcery in clear language, and free from some of the barriers and obfuscation with which it has been clouded, it will be of benefit to those who dare to tread a path that leads quickly to both wisdom and power.

Gender and Sexual Orientation

I am yet another straight male, in a long line of straight males, writing on sex magic. Most of what I write about in this book can be applied by anyone of any gender or sexual orientation, but some of it will have to be interpreted, and some of it may not be applicable to everyone. There will also be practices that are not covered in the book because I have not been taught them and have not experimented with them.

When it comes to gender, it is no secret that the bulk of sex magic material has been written for males. Patriarchy is certainly the overriding reason for this, but there are also technical considerations:

1. Men are apt to reach orgasm faster than women—much too fast for most sex magic operations.
2. Men release their sexual fluids, and this can have a draining effect on energy.
3. Men are not prone to multiple orgasms.

In short, there is more sex magic instruction for men because men need more instruction.

Many books talk a lot about gender polarities as if anything and everything about men and women is completely different. This is mirrored in some traditional teachings as well, but I find in reality it is not the case. For the most part the magic in this book does not rely upon anyone having to fulfill expectations of what it means to be a "real man" or "real woman." I also avoid speaking about "men who run feminine energy" and other similar terms that try so hard to make the multifaceted spectrum of behavior and energy fit into one of two slots. Whether you are cisgendered or transgendered, everything in this book should be workable. You are the best judge of what you can and should do with the information in the book, not me.

During the writing of the book I have been asked several times if I am covering homosexual sex magic. The answer is that apart from a few pieces of history and tradition, and a few ideas for practice sprinkled throughout, there is not much *specific* to homosexual magic or sex in the book. One reason is that much of the magic is not dependent upon male-female coupling. Techniques of inner heat, of unlocking innate divinity, of riding the wave of ego-shattering energy of the orgasm has nothing at all to do with sexual orientation. Formulas that do rely upon male–female coupling, such as the creation of the Elixir, are not for me to change. Just as there are specific magics to heterosexual union that may not apply in homosexual union, there are also formulas that apply in homosexual union that do not apply in heterosexual union. Not being homosexual, it is not my place to present those mysteries. Sadly, much of the history of homosexual sacred sexuality and sex magic has been kept underground or repressed. Thankfully I know of a few good sources for investigation as well as some promising works being released in the near future. Keep an eye on my blog, *www.inominandum.com/blog.*

Consent and Coercion

Any sexual act, regardless of whether it is part of sex sorcery, should be consented to by two adults that are capable of making decisions. Any acts that involve someone forced or coerced, someone under the influence of intoxicants to the point that he or she cannot exercise sound judgment, someone under the legal age of consent, or anyone not expressing enthusiastic and clear consent should be considered antithetical to the work.

As far as I am concerned, any acts between consenting adults that do not cause harm to anyone involved are okay by me.

CHAPTER 1

A *Story from the East and a Story from the West*

Spiritual stories are important. Stories and myths have an ability to convey meaning on multiple levels at once, as well as place sometimes odd beliefs and practices into a useful context within our particular culture and the world at large. Before we delve into the factual history, theory, and practice of sex magic I want to share two stories that illustrate the role and importance of erotic magic. One story is from the East and another one is from the West, and each has had a deep impact on the mystery traditions of its respective hemisphere.

A Story from the East

The Guhyasamāja is one of the earliest tantras in existence. Dating from the 3rd or 4th century and attributed to the Siddha Asanga, this text is one of the first in Buddhist Literature to extol the virtues of sensory pleasure as a path to enlightenment. The story of how the teaching came into existence is a curious one that involved a Buddha and a King...

It is said that King Indrabhuti, ruler of the country of Uddhiyana in what is now Afghanistan, observed a strange phenomena every night and every morning: a flock of yellow birds that travelled north into the Himalayas at night, and south back to India every morning. The king consulted his ministers on the odd pattern the birds were taking, and they informed him that they were not birds at all, but the Buddha and 500 Arhats all dressed in yellow robes. They would fly to Mt. Kailash in the evening to practice meditation in the solitude of the holy mountain, and fly back to Varanasi in the morning in order to teach the Dharma.

The king, being impressed by this, decided to invite the Buddha to teach in his kingdom. The next day he arranged a massive Puja with heaps of offerings and hundreds of prayers. The Buddha appeared along with his retinue of 500 yellow-robed Arhats. The Buddha then began to teach on what most of us think of as Buddhism: the need for renunciation, abstaining from intoxicants, the benefits of meditation, and of course the value of monastic celibacy.

After a few days of this manner of teaching, King Indrabhuti protested that it was all well and good to renounce the world and become a monk, but that he could not possibly do it. He was responsible for the wellbeing of his kingdom, the raising of his many children, and of course the happiness of the queen, whom we assume would be upset if the king were to suddenly abandon sex with her. The king asked if there was not another way to attain enlightenment, one that did not abandon sensory enjoyment.

The Buddha smiled at this request and transformed himself into the glorious Guhyasamāja, a being of many arms and heads who sat on a lotus seat in sexual union with a woman who also had many arms and heads. They were in turn surrounded by a mandala of other beings doing the same. Because they were very pure monks, the 500 Arhats who attended the Buddha, as well as all the others in the palace, fainted, which explains why the events are not recalled in the Sutras. The Buddha then taught the king the method of secret conduct, which involves using passions that are ordinarily thought of as poisons and alchemically transforming them into the basis of enlightenment itself.

The king and his wife practiced the Guhyasamāja Tantra and attained enlightenment in their own lifetime, a difficult if not impossible task with the Sutric teachings. The king taught the tantric method to all his subjects, who also became fully enlightened, thus depopulating the country of Uddhiyana. Before the inhabitants of the kingdom became beings of light, however, the king wrote down the tantra and concealed it in a stupa. A sea formed around the stupa and became filled with Nagas (serpent people) who also became enlightened through the method of the tantra. A thousand years later the great Mahasiddha Nagarjuna came across this sea and was allowed by the Nagas to open the stupa and take the text back with him to India.

This story is mirrored very closely in the Kalachakra Tantra. Here it was at the request of King Suchandra, who was from the kingdom of Shambhala, and the Buddha taught it to him as a way of attaining enlightenment that did not require him abandoning his 50 wives! The king took it back to Shambhala (the famous hidden kingdom that has fascinated both East and West, inspiring the stories of Shangri-La from James Hilton's *Lost Horizon*, as well as being the location of Madame Blavatsky's Great White Lodge in her theosophical teachings). The Kalachakra Tantra contains prophesies about the Kingdom of Shambhala: it says the kingdom will come back into phase with our reality sometime around 2424 AD and lead a huge army to vanquish evil forces and usher in a new Golden Age of humanity.

Whatever the merits of such prophesies, it is amusing to wonder if the thousands of people to whom the Dalai Lama gives the Kalachakra initiation each year, who walk away with six-session Guru Yoga prayers, ever dig deep enough to know that, at its core, it is a bedroom practice.

The point of this story, in whichever version you hear it, is to convey a spiritual truth. In this case the takeaway, in my opinion, should be that there is an outer teaching and an inner teaching, which sometimes contradict each other, but which ultimately lead to the same state. The outer teachings tend to be outer teachings because they are easier to understand, can be worked by most people, and are safer than the inner teachings. The inner teachings are meant for special people, thus in both the Guhyasamāja and Kalachakra versions, the person receiving the teaching is a king. In the inner teaching, sex and the other passions that might ordinarily lead one into further materialistic grasping and suffering can be applied through Ghuyacharya, secret conduct, and become a medicine precisely for those things.

The practitioners of the outer teachings will deny the efficacy of this approach. Some are not even aware of its existence. That is okay, and perhaps as it should be. But as monasticism and renunciation seem to be becoming less and less attractive in both the East and the West, some feel that it is time for the inner teachings to become more widespread and lead to a new definition of what spirituality actually entails.

A Story from the West

Chances are that unless you are entirely new to the concept of sex magic, you know that Aleister Crowley practiced it as part of his religious and philosophical system known as Thelema—a Greek word meaning "will and desire." Crowley was inspired by Francois Rabelais, who wrote about an Abbey of Thelema in his book *Gargantua and Pantagruel* nearly 400 years before Crowley established his own version of such an abbey in Cefalu, Sicily, in 1920. What fewer people know is that Rabelais's use of the term was most likely inspired by a chapter within one of the most enigmatic books of Western literature: *The Hypnerotomachia Poliphili*, which translates as "Polifilo's Strife of Love in a Dream."[1] This book was printed anonymously in Venice in 1499 and uses a very difficult linguistic style that is a combination of Italian, Greek, and Latin. It is attributed to Francesco Colonna because the first letter of each chapter spells out POLIAM FRATER FRANCISCVS COLVMNA PERAMAVIT, which translates as "Brother Francesco Colonna has dearly loved Polia." Most believe that this reveals the author to be a Dominican monk who preached at San Marco Cathedral during the time that the book was published. Some scholars believe that the book was written by a different Colonna who was a Roman Governor at the time, and yet others attribute it to the famous Lorenzo de Medici.

The book recounts the tale of a man named Poliphilo, which can loosely be translated as "lover of all things," and his search for his true love, Polia, or "all things." The quest takes him through ancient temples, secret lakes and alcoves, enchanted forests, and mysterious portals. All through the book he marvels and waxes poetic about the beauty he finds not only in the many women and nymphs he meets, but also in the architecture, landscape, and sculptures he encounters. Truly a love of *all* things. At one point he encounters the Queen Eleuterylida (loosely translated as "free will"), who instructs him to choose between three portals to continue his quest. To lead him to these portals, the queen assigns two nymphs: Logistica (reason or logic) and Thelemia (will or desire). A long journey ensues, during which Logistica offers lots of explanation and advice to Poliphilo, while Thelemia says little by comparison. Eventually they arrive at an impenetrable pass where three brazen portals are carved into the side of the living rock. Each portal is marked with an inscription in Arabic, Hebrew, Greek, and Latin (see the image on the next page).

The first portal is marked with the words *Gloria Dei* in Latin, *Theodoxia* in Greek, *Tif'eret ha-El* in Hebrew, and *Jal Allah* in Arabic. These all translate to "Glory of God." The three travelers knock on the portal and a shriveled old matron dressed in rags comes out to greet them. The road through this portal is stony and covered in thorns and brambles. Logistica, seeing that Poliphilo was not interested in this portal, tried to encourage him to take it, saying, "This path is not known until the end is reached." Thelemia, however, advised him, "O Poliphilo, the love of this laborious woman is not yet for you."

They knock on the second portal, which is marked with the words *Gloria Mundi* in Latin, *Cosmodoxia* in Greek, *Tif'ret ha-Olam* in Hebrew, and *Jal Ad-Dinya* in Arabic. These all translate to "Glory of the World." They are again greeted by a matron, but this time she is strong, with powerful arms, and holds a golden sword with a

This illustration is from the *Hypnerotomachia Poliphili* by Francesco Colanna

From *https://archive.org/details/hypnerotoocolluoft*

crown and palm branch suspended from it. She and her maiden attendants radiate the strength that is only developed after prevailing in combat and trial. Logistica begins to sing a song in praise of this path: " O Poliphilo, do not shrink from the manly combat of this place, for when the labour is past, the reward remains." Her song is so vehement that Poliphilo is ready to walk through this portal and face whatever trial awaits. Thelemia caresses him and gently reminds him, "It seems sensible, Poliphilo my pet, that before you stay here you should at least look at the third portal."

The third portal is marked with the words *Mater Amoris* in Latin, *Erototrophos* in Greek, *Gidul ha-Ahava* in Hebrew, and *Um el-Muja-ba* in Arabic. The meaning of these is "Mother of Love" or "Nurturer of Love." Once in the portal they are met by a joyful young woman whose wanton gaze captures the attention of Poliphilo immediately.

The path behind her is a voluptuous garden overflowing with abundant beauty, food, drink, and of course nymphs. Logistica warns Poliphilo not to be sucked in by "a feigned and cosmetic beauty, deceitful, insipid, and vain." She warns that there will be heartbreak and pain and death and all manner of disappointment and poison if he takes this path. Logistica goes on and on like this for some time, but Thelemia simply glances at him and makes a gesture that he should not listen to Logistica. Logistica gets angry, throws down her Lyre, and runs off. Thelemia assures Poliphilo, "This is the place, Poliphilo, where it will surely not be long before you find the thing you love most, the thing that is yours, the one thing in the world which your obstinate heart unceasingly thinks about and hopes for."

So Poliphilo, led by the coquettish women, passes through this portal, where, after a short rest, he resumes his quest. Eventually he finds Polia, who rebukes him, causing him to die. Polia is then encouraged by the Goddess Venus herself to love Poliphilo, so she returns and kisses him, which returns him to life. She and Poliphilo resolve to devote themselves to love and the works of love. They embrace, Polia disappears, and Poliphilo wakes up from his dream.

This story represents the first use of the term *Thelema* to indicate a path that represents the personal will, as opposed to the will of an external god as a spiritual path.[2] It specifically rejects the idea that one needs to choose between a life of renouncing passion and pleasure to know god, represented by the Theodoxia gate, or a purely material life driven by success, power, and conquest, represented by the Cosmodoxia gate. Instead one can embrace passion and pleasure and eventually come to know Polia—All Things.

***

These two stories represent a subtle teaching on the philosophy behind sexual magic, and the place it holds in the greater scheme of spirituality. Both stories represent a path that can lead to realization faster than paths of renunciation and asceticism. They also represent paths that can be hazardous: Logistica was not wrong about the dangers of the third gate, and there is a reason that the

Buddha was not teaching the Guhyasamāja Tantra widely in India, or even to the 500 Arhats that accompanied him.

Despite the dangers, though, in Indrabhuti the Buddha saw a sovereign who could handle the teaching and really could attain enlightenment in no other way. Thelemia saw the same in Poliphilo. There are many who feel that the old ways of religious asceticism are no longer the most appropriate method of spiritual expression for our planet. Simple materialism has also failed us, and seems to bring us further and further from real fulfillment and realization as a species. The first and second gates have failed. Perhaps it is time to walk through the third.

CHAPTER 2

The Perils of Passion:
The Dangers of Sexual Sorcery

One thing we are told in both the East and the West is that sexual spirituality is dangerous. Critics from outside the practice warn of everything from simple moral decay to demonic possession. Even if we throw out these puritanical and monastic warnings about sex, we are still left with the fact that even practitioners of sexual magic usually acknowledge that there is an element of danger.

In the Buddhist tantras we are warned that it is like climbing up the cliff face of a mountain rather than taking the slow and winding path. It leads to enlightenment faster, but it is much easier to lose footing on a cliff than a path, and the drop can be fatal. When evaluating the real dangers of this path we are left with a strange situation. On the one hand, sexual practice allegedly harnesses awesome powers so great that it can lead one to ruin or madness when mishandled. On the other hand, sex is something that most people do on a fairly regular basis, so how dangerous can it really be?

Sex and Morality

Because you are reading this book and are therefore interested in doing sex magic, sex yoga, or sexual spiritual practice, you are probably not someone who thinks of sex as dirty, bad, or evil, but many people have and many people do. It was not long ago that in the West anything outside of heterosexual sex within the bonds of marriage and only for purposes of procreation was considered taboo by society. Although some people still hold these strict views, and others selectively condemn certain types of sex, overall our society today is pretty open to any kind of sexual activity between consenting adults. Today most of you reading this live in places where homosexuality, polyamory, masturbation, kink, and so on, although perhaps not embraced by society as a whole, are not exactly shocking. Given modern technology and travel it is easier than ever to find support and partners for just about any activity you can imagine, and pornography that caters to it.[1]

Despite this, some people still insist that sex magic should be written about in code or kept secret because it is too shocking. It is certainly true that 400 years ago one might have been burned at the stake for it, and just 100 years ago women might have collapsed with vapors at the thought of it, but I submit that in the era of "2Girls1Cup," nothing in this book or the annals of sexual practice in the East or the West can be so shocking that we need to encode it anymore. Certainly the idea that still persists in some circles, that sex magic is just an excuse for people to have sex, can be dismissed immediately: people have never needed an excuse to have sex.

STDs and Pregnancy

I would hope that everyone reading this has a firm grasp of what STDs are, such HIV/AIDS, Hetetitus, HPV, and so on. I would also hope that everyone reading this knows that sex can get you pregnant. I would hope that everyone knows that condoms are the best protection against both STDs and unwanted pregnancy. The problem is that, amazingly, many people still don't know these facts.

Worse yet, many people believe that doing sex magic will somehow shield them from both disease and unwanted pregnancy. I assure you that it will not. Please take every precaution to maintain good health. The spirits, the energy, and your general "magicalness" will not stop you from getting a serious disease.

Because semen retention is taught in this book, and because in the past it has been used as a form of birth control, some people think that if you do not release semen you cannot get someone pregnant. This is only the case if you are an absolute *master* and are using Vajroli techniques[2] the whole time. You are not a master yet. Not for years. People relied upon this method for birth control when there was no other reliable means. You, however, are living in the 21st century, not the 4th.

Certain acts in the book, those concerned with inner energy work and using the orgasmic state as a gateway to visions and gnosis, are not hampered by the use of a condom. Others, that rely upon the mixing of sexual fluids, are. Please understand that you should take every precaution to make sure that you and your partner get tested for STDs, and unless you want a child, use other methods of birth control.

Talk to your doctor about any confusion you have on any of these issues. Nothing in this book is intended as medical advice.

Sex and Control

One reason that sex has been treated as dirty or dangerous is because doing so enables churches and other entities to use it as a method of control and manipulation. Whether controlling a populace, a small cult, or a single person in a relationship, sex is a potent tool for forcing people into submission.

When you preach that the only means of having sex without risking eternal damnation is getting married by a priest, the organization that oversees marriage has a lot of power, as well as the ability to make a lot of money. Celibacy was forced on Catholic priests in the 11th century not as a means of keeping Christ-like, but as a method for stopping the children of priests from inheriting property that otherwise might go to the church.

In Tibet there were times when monks and High Lamas persecuted the married tantric priests on claims that they were immoral. Just as with the Catholic Church though, one could make a compelling argument that in a country where the government was synonymous with the monastic system, married Lamas offering a path to enlightenment that did not require celibacy presented a threat to both the numbers of potential monks to fill the monastery and the financial support they garner from the populace.

In smaller cults sex can be used more directly as a type of mind control. The list of groups that have been accused of using sex as a way to attract and control converts is long: Branch Davidians, Rajneesh, the Sai Baba Movement, Heaven's Gate, Raeliens, and The Family International are just the most famous. The very primal power that makes sex so useful a tool in magic and spirituality is also what makes it useful for controlling people.

Even in groups that do an admirable job overall of conducting themselves in a responsible way regarding sexual practice, there will be individuals who do not. For example, I spent many years in the Ordo Templi Orientis (OTO), a group that uses sexually charged symbolism in its rites and teaches sexual magic at the higher levels. Overall I was, and remain, impressed at the manner in which the organization and the vast majority of its initiates handle themselves. I did, however, encounter a few individuals who would exploit the teachings for their own ends. Women were told that to be a real Scarlett Woman they should make themselves available to anyone; others were promised inner teachings that could only be transmitted during sex. I also know of men who were told the same type of things: a genuine Therion should be ready to have sex with anyone or be ready to switch orientation. The people I encountered who did this were almost always of a lower degree and not the leaders of the organization. Still it is worth noting that where there is sacred sex or sex magic, there are unscrupulous people who are willing to use it to control others.

To sum it up: *don't do things you are not comfortable with*. If you are in a group or with a teacher who views all women or all men as "naturally" having either a submissive or dominant role, leave. If you are with a teacher who wants you to have sex in a way that is counter to your sexual orientation, leave. If your teacher insists on having sex as part of the teaching method, leave. If a teacher tells you that you are his or hers from a former life, that he or she has been waiting for you, or any other kind of trip like that, leave.

Of course, there is nothing wrong with any of these activities as long as you *want* to engage in them. It can be very fulfilling, enlightening, and empowering to be a submissive or dominant, to stretch the bounds of your programming by having sex outside of your natural orientation, or even to have sex as part of the teaching/learning method, as long as *you want to*. If you want to, don't let anyone stop you. If you don't want to, don't let anyone force or coerce you.

Pumping up the Volume

Once we navigate the dangers we face from others while attempting to learn sex magic, we are left with the dangers sex practice poses to ourselves. Sadly, this is an area where people tend to err toward the extremes. On the one hand some people will say that sex magic is incredibly dangerous and should only be attempted by people with decades of other types of spiritual practice behind them or who have been specially gifted from birth. On the other hand we have proponents of sexual sorcery who write off all warnings as the product of puritanical values or fearful prudes, and insist that there is no danger to sexual magic at all.

We can dismiss the warnings about needing to be highly trained or born enlightened in order to practice. In Buddhist circles you have many students and teachers alike who preach that it is dangerous to practice sex yogas with a physical partner unless you are a Tulku (a reincarnated lama) or a great Mahasiddha, but this ignores the specific injunctions in texts that stress that practicing tantra with a partner is not only recommended but *necessary* for people of low or medium capacity; working with visualized consorts alone is for people of highest capacity.

We should also dismiss the idea that there is no danger by the fact that almost every source on the subject in the East and the West warns that there is danger. It is not a matter of there being no risk, it is a matter of the risks being overblown and the rewards more than worth whatever risk there is.

The real dangers that sexual magic poses to the practitioner are the same as with any type of work that increases the amount of energy we channel: everything going on in our mind and body increases. This means that the sense of primordial bliss, divinity, and non-duality we experience from the energy work that follows increases. It means the ability to manifest reality with magic also increases. This is why we do the work. Unfortunately it also means that undesirable qualities and attachments also increase; this is the real danger. When Eastern texts speak of "ego-clinging" we might dismiss it if we are approaching the practice from a more occult perspective, but what that means is that every part of the ego is gaining strength, including unhealthy passions. There is nothing inherently wrong with passion. Passion is life and power and the root of great joy. It can also be the root of great suffering when things are thrown out of balance. This is how healthy lust turns to rape, how anger turns to assault and murder, and how ignorance turns to blind hate and fear. Any kind of serious energy work or internal alchemy turns the volume up on *everything* that goes on in our stream of being, not just the parts we would like. Sex practice takes that basic energy practice and brings it to a whole new level of potency. As the rewards increase, so do the risks.

In today's world where we have readily available hyper-stimuli of violent movies, pornography, and all sorts of new mental input, the danger of escalating the passions in undesired and even violent ways is increased beyond anything our ancestors faced. I am not against pornography or violent movies, mind you; both have their place. I am simply stating that it is up to the individual to monitor their effect on the psyche. When engaged in energetic and sex practices that stoke the internal fires higher, this need is even greater.

Physical Dangers

On top of the risks faced by the mental and energetic body, the physical body is also susceptible to dangers of the path. For example, some types of breath work can trigger heart palpitations and lightheadedness. Certain traditional positions might be strenuous or damaging to people with different conditions.

Some changes in the brain also tend to take place during meditation and magic that some have found unsettling. For example, in many meditators, activity in the parietal lobe, which controls the sense of boundary and personal space, decreases dramatically. Meanwhile, activity in the frontal lobe, which controls analysis, increases. The combination makes you hyper-aware (frontal) that your boundaries between self and other are breaking down (parietal). In the vast majority of people this is a positive experience, and the scientific studies on meditation, yoga, and prayer on the brain show very positive changes overall. It is important to be aware, though, that a very small minority of people have found these changes unsettling and in rare cases they have been reported to exacerbate mental stress.

In both these cases the best prevention is common sense: you know what you are capable of. If you are 80 pounds overweight, don't try the sex position where you are standing on one foot with the other raised straight up. If you have knee trouble, don't worry about sitting in full lotus—use a chair. If you are terrified of darkness or are claustrophobic, don't work with blindfolds and bondage. There is nothing in this book that you *have* to do. Only things that you can do if you want.

It should also go without saying that seeing a doctor, a psychiatrist, or whatever other medical care you require is a good idea. Nothing in any of my books is meant to be a replacement for medical or psychological treatment.

Purification

Now that we have spoken of the dangers and some of the common-sense ways to prevent them, it's time to talk about an important but often overlooked aspect of not only sex sorcery, but of magic in general: purification. The type of purification we are talking about here has nothing to do with sin against a god, or things to feel guilty about, or anything like that. Quite the opposite, in fact. It has to do with freedom and clarity. Acts of purification are essential in eliminating some of the dangers we will face in the work ahead.

Think of yourself as a lake that is constantly agitated by storms and turbulence. You cannot see the bottom of the lake because there is dirt and such always being tossed about in the water. If we can somehow stop that agitation and still the water, the dirt settles and the water is revealed as inherently *pure* and clear. The turbulence is the mental, emotional, energetic, and physical turbulence of daily life. The clarity is the natural state of your mind.

The idea of purification is an essential part of almost all magical systems the world over. Solomonic magicians spend several days bathing and praying intensely to purify themselves before major operations. Tantric Buddhists accumulate hundreds of thousands of Vajrasattva mantras in order to purify body, speech, and mind before embarking on serious tantric training. Shamans spend periods detoxing and purifying themselves before vision quests. Because sex magic draws specifically on the most passionate and charged aspects of our mind and body, this purification is even more vital than in other endeavors.

Outer, Inner, and Secret Purification

When Dudjom Rinpoche taught about the different methods of purification in the different vehicles of Dharma, he would use the analogy of a poisonous plant in a yard, to show the differences in method between the Buddhist Yanas. In the following paragraphs I have reworded it so that it is more universally applicable.

The outer method of purification is renunciation, avoiding the poisonous plant entirely. This is the path that monks and nuns take. You know that certain passions can distract from clarity, so you avoid them as much as you possibly can. It is said to be the easiest route to enlightenment, but it takes a very long time. This may or may not be true; for all I know it may really be the best route. All I know is that it is not the route for me, and if you are taking my courses, I am pretty sure that it is not the route for you either.

The inner method is that of the antidote. In this way you accept that you are not avoiding the poisonous plant, but are instead seeking to negate its effects with other actions. This is the path that most non-renunciates take. They feel anger so they concentrate on peace. They feel envy so they concentrate on non-attachment. The idea is that you spend your time routing every negative quality and cultivating positive qualities. This is excellent but difficult work that also can take a very long time. The problem is that we all have innumerable qualities and can spend lifetimes doing this. It also can lead to legalistic spiritual thinking, such that we judge positive and negatives, seeking some balance that is never really attained. You can see this in afterlife scenarios from Maat weighing the heart, to Catholic ideas of hell, heaven, and purgatory.

The secret method is that of alchemical transformation. In this case the plant in our analogy gets used to make the Elixir of Life. Passions like anger, ignorance, lust, sloth, and so on have great energy behind them; this is what gives them so much power in our lives. This energy is also what makes them an extremely potent tool for transformation. This is the reason you are reading this book.

Breath Purification

Moving from the outer to the inner, it is equally important to cleanse the vital channels. I wrote about the nine breath purifications in my book *The Sorcerer's Secrets*, and that is the method I still use on a daily basis. To do this, draw in a deep breath through both nostrils, and as you do so consider that the air coming in is pure and cleansing. As you inhale, draw your right arm up at your side so that it is held straight out; this will open up the right channel that handles solar and masculine forces. With your arm still held out at your side, bend your elbow so that your hand is in front of your face, and block your right nostril with your finger. Exhale forcefully through your left nostril, visualizing all impure energies and tendencies leaving the body through the left side.

Do the exact same thing again, but using the left arm and blocking the left nostril this time, exhaling through the right nostril. Repeat the process twice more for each side, making six breaths in total. For the last three breaths simply breathe in and out through both nostrils, cleaning out the central channel. You should again visualize pure air being inhaled and impure air being exhaled. As you exhale, lean forward as far as is possible to force the last bit of air out of the channel.

The White Star Purification Meditation

The following exercise rests on the invocation of higher powers to pour their energy and divine nectar to and through us. Those of you who have taken Tantric Buddhist initiation will note the similarities to the Vajrasattva Sadhanas that inspired the practice.

STEP 1: Begin with the breath purification I just described, and follow it with a seated meditation of a few minutes.

STEP 2: Visualize a star above your head. Arising from the star you should see two beings emerge: a god and goddess. I see them as pure white, naked and nameless. You can see them adorned as an appropriate god and goddess pair if you so choose, but I choose to keep them unadorned. However you see them, they must be in sexual embrace. Regardless of your sexual orientation, you should still see them as male and female. Remember, this is a work of purification, not passion. It is the idea of combined polarities that is important here.

Above the heads of the pair is an infinite field of every being that has ever attained enlightenment, gnosis, or spiritual ascension throughout all times and places. Beneath your seat is a pit that houses a realm of demons and suffering.

STEP 3: To begin the purification proper you should make a mental confession to the god and goddess pair arising from your star center. They act as intermediaries to the college of beings that have attained full realization. This confession should not be based on any kind of rigid code or commandments, but is rather an admission of ways that you have fallen from your own ideals and allowed your own mind to be obscured.

Consider that the deity pair at your crown transmits your confession to the enlightenment field above their head and that in response, lights of blessing and purification shine down upon the deity pair.

STEP 4: That deity pair engage in sexual union and filter the subtle beams of light from the enlightenment field into their sexual fluids. That elixir in turn runs down into your central channel and filters throughout your body. It impregnates and purifies all your cells, subtle channels, and thought processes. As you fill with nectar you should visualize that black, inky gook starts flowing from your body. You should take a moment to focus on this black oil leaving your eyes, purifying sight; leaving your nose, purifying smell; leaving your mouth, purifying taste and speech; leaving your ears, purifying hearing; leaving your groin, purifying sexual grasping; and finally leaving through all your pores, purifying your whole body at once.

First the nectar pushes everything out in a downward cleansing, and you should focus on everything flowing out of you in a downward motion. This eventually gives way to the nectar filling you and rising in your body, yielding an upward cleansing motion whereby you see the black oil coming out of your eyes and nose and such. Lastly there is the instantaneous cleansing of the mind, which is negativity being cast away like darkness cast away by switching on a light.

As you meditate this way, you can repeat the mantra ELAYABARA, which is a phrase for harnessing the combined essence of the elements that I received during a communication from the elemental spirits.

STEP 5: See all the black oil flowing down from you into the demon-filled pit below. This is not a punishment to those beings; it is a gift. Just as the sexual runoff of the deity pair is precious elixir and nectar to you, so is your runoff as nectar to beings in a more gross and grasping state.

When you feel as though you have done all you can, you can simply thank all beings involved, vow to attempt to maintain purity and clarity, and move on.

CHAPTER 3

The Subtle Body Laid Bare:
Channels, Centers, and Drops

A good deal of sex magic involves manipulating the physical, etheric, and astral bodies. Before we can do that, we first have to know the lay of the land: the anatomy of the subtle body.

In my book *The Sorcerer's Secrets* I talk about the spectrum that exists between the dense material world and the increasingly subtle world of spirit. In the book we deal with three levels:

Level 3: The Material Body

Level 2: The Aetherial/Etheric Body

Level 1: The Empyrian/Astral Body

This roughly corresponds to the Body, Namshe, and Lha of Tibet; the physical body, ti bon ang, and gros bon ang of Vodou; The Body, Soul, and Spirit of St. Paul; and the Material, Astral, and Akashic Bodies of Bardon's system. And there are other ways to break this spectrum down:

In Khabbalah the four main bodies are the Neschema or Divine Body, Ruach or Mind Body, the Nephesh or astral body, and the Guf or Physical body. In some types of Hinduism there are five sheaths that are spoken of: the Annamayakosha, or the sheath of food, which is the physical body; the Pranamayakosha, or the sheath of breath, which corresponds to the higher biological and lower astral levels; the Manomayakosha, or sheath of mind, which is the intellect and the ego; the Vijnanamayakosha, which is the sheath of subtle mind and controls higher-level and transcendent functions; and finally the Anandamayakosha, the sheath of bliss, which refers to the highest and causal level of the body that is perfectly divine and transcendent.

I mention all these scenarios because I want you to realize that they are all true, just expressing different things in different ways. The divisions are made based upon the needs of the system, so there is no need to argue the truth of one over another. In this book I don't want to add too many levels, but it is necessary to speak specifically about a level that exists between the material and astral bodies: the etheric body.

First let's start with the material body.

The Material Body

This is the physical body of flesh, bones, blood, nerves, glands, and so on. In most magic, the physical body takes a back seat to the mind and energy. Not so in sex sorcery. In this work the physical body will play a major role, and rather than relying upon the mind and spirit to influence the physical world, we will often be relying upon the physical to influence the higher levels. Energy in the physical body has to be moved along through purely physical means such as organs pumping, food digesting, and so on.

The Etheric Body

This body is right on the border between the astral and the material. It is the etheric body that contains the channels, drops, chakras, and other subtle body organs that can be manipulated by psychic healers, acupuncturists, martial artists, and others. Unlike the astral body, the etheric body cannot move more than an inch or two from the physical body. Its structures are closely mirrored to physical body structures: channels relate to nerves, chakras relate to glands, and drops relate to sexual fluids, as we shall see in the next section. Energy moving through the etheric body is directed by a combination of physical and astral-level work: breath and muscle move in conjunction with focus and will.

The Astral Body

This is the classical subtle body that people usually experience during an out of body experience. It is termed "astral" because it is able to separate from the physical body and travel on its own to the starry realms.[1] The structures of the etheric body are connected to this level, but in a more mutable state. The astral body can change shape and allow the magician to take on god forms for invocation, or to travel in animal form, such as the famous Benedanti of Italy or some modern-day lycanthropic magical groups. The tendency, however, is for the astral body to take a shape that mimics a slightly idealized version of your physical self. Energy in the astral body can be moved purely through will, focus, and imagination. It can move within or outside of the body and is not limited to channels and such.

Etheric Body Anatomy

Because the anatomy of the physical body is quite well known and the structures of the astral body are so subtle and shifting, it is the etheric body to which we must turn our focus. This is where the lion's share of sex magic happens. As I said earlier, the etheric body is the densest of the nonphysical bodies, and, just like the physical body, has its own veins, organs, and biology. Some systems of studying the nonphysical bodies have extremely detailed maps of the etheric and astral bodies showing thousands of channels, chakras, sub-chakras, and so on. One chart I have on my shelf here shows the location of 72,000 channels in the subtle body. Whereas these very detailed maps are useful for acupuncturists and skilled traditional healers, focusing on that amount of detail can actually be a distraction when trying to work with the etheric body.

For our work here there are three factors that we need to be aware of: the channels, the seeds or drops, and the chakras. Chakras are a popular topic in modern occultism, but in traditional yoga, tantra, qi gung, and other subtle body disciplines they are actually not as important as the channels that connect them.

Variations and Tradition

Before we get deeper into specifics I want to take a moment to state that there is no definitive teaching on anything that follows. Even within the same tradition, different teachings and teachers will give various details in different ways. Some texts talk about seven Chakras, some talk about only four, and others work with nine. Some texts say the central channel is as wide as a straw, others as large as a finger width, and yet others claim it is as thin as a blade of grass. Some say you need to see inner flame sparked by four eggs, others claim it needs to be sparked by visualizing the letter RAM in Sanskrit. What I present is something that is accessible to everybody of just about any culture or tradition, and focuses on essentials so that you do not get bogged down in a dozen different details.

If you are familiar with chakras, nadis, meridians, gates, and other subtle body structures, but don't see a particular chakra or channel covered here, that is because I am focusing only on what we need to know for the teachings in this book. It is a deep subject and the Bibliography will provide a great start for further research.

Channels

The Central Channel

This is the most important channel in the body; in *The Sorcerer's Secrets* I refer to it as "The Pillar." In Sanskrit it is called the Avadhuti or the Shushumna. It starts at the top of the head, at the point where the skull plates join, and terminates at the perineum. It is the central collection point for energies in the body. Variations of color, size, and the exact points of termination differ from tradition to tradition. For instance, some have the channel terminating at the head of the penis or the vagina and beginning at the third eye.

The Right and Left Channels

These run on the left and right sides of the central channel and are fairly close to it. They are also called the solar and lunar channels, or male and female channels. They are sometimes shown spinning or spiraling around the central channel like a strand of DNA, but mostly are shown as running alongside the central channel. The solar channel is on the right and lunar channel is on the left, and they relate to the elements of Fire and Water, respectively. They also relate to the left brain and right brain (right channel = left brain; left channel = right brain). Hindu and Buddhist yogas do a lot of work with these channels as they govern most inner experiences. The central channel and two side channels are called "The Thrusting Channels" in Chi Kung. They connect to the central channel at the perineum and the crown of the head and have sub channels that extend to the nostrils, eyes, arms, legs, and all throughout the body.

The Front and Rear Channels

These are called the functioning and governing channels in Chi Kung, and run up the front and rear of the body. The rear channel starts at the base of the central channel at the perineum, runs up the rear of the body into the brain, and then down the front of the face, terminating in the mouth. The front channel extends from the tip of the tongue down the front of the body and meets the central channel again at the perineum. Some descriptions have the rear channel ending at the crown and the front channel descending from the crown to the perineum. Regardless of the specifics, the channels connect when you move the tip of the tongue to the top of the mouth. Generally, energy circulates up the rear and down the front, though this can be reversed. Those familiar with Chi Kung will know this as the Microcosmic Energy Orbit and can attest to the feelings of strength and wellness that arise when these channels are strengthened through work.

We will not be using the front and rear channels much in this work, but those who explore further into Taoist Inner Alchemy will be relying upon them heavily, so I thought it was important to note that they are all a part of the same map.

The Belt Channel

The belt channel also runs from the crown to the perineum, but does so in an outer spiral around all the other channels. This channel provides the natural defenses for the body and can be strengthened with shields, reverse breathing, and other defensive measures. In sex magic the belt channels of two people interact and merge energies. Defenses are laid down and two become one.

The Limb Channels

From the left and right channels extend channels that go into the arms. They terminate in the palms and then have five extensions into the fingers, relating to the five elements. Traditional sources for which finger relates to which element vary widely, even within the same tradition. For instance, in Tibetan Buddhism the Kalachakra Tantra says the thumb is earth, in Guhyasamāja it is space, and in the Bon Ma-Gyud it is water. I have experimented with this and have been able to channel any element down any channel equally, so the point is moot from a practical perspective. What I will say is that the index and middle fingers draw energy gathered from above with greater ease, and the ring and little fingers gather from below. You can experiment with this yourself by holding your arms out at your sides and seeing how much more stable you are when concentrating on your ring and little finger than on your index and middle. You can even have someone try to move you while doing this to see the difference; it is really quite striking.

There are also limb channels that extend from the perineum down through the legs and terminate in the feet. These are not to be neglected. When you do a practice like the Pillar and Spheres, in which you draw up energy from below while standing, you are actually drawing it up through both legs, allowing it to gather in the perineum and then ascending through the central channel.

The importance of limb channels in sex magic should be obvious—you are, after all, touching and feeling with the hands and entwining limbs.

Power Centers

Located along the channels are centers that gather, pattern, and recirculate the energy of the body. These are most often thought of as wheels or chakras. You are probably already thinking of the seven chakras, because most of what has been written in the West about chakras has come from the handful of texts translated into English more than 100 years ago by people like Walter Evans-Wentz and Arthur Avalon (Sir John Woodroffe), who first presented the idea of seven chakras. In fact, chakras are so present in Western occult literature that for a while you could scarcely find a book on witchcraft or ceremonial magic that did not have a section on chakras—whether it had anything to do with the subject or not. But there is a lot more to working with the etheric, astral, and other bodies than just these power points, which is why I wanted to bring attention to the channels first. In my experience, focusing on the channels and the movement of different types of energy through the various main channels of the body is more useful than focusing on the

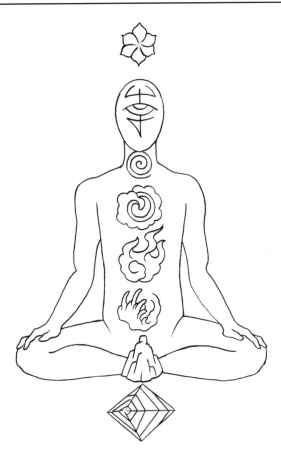

chakras right out of the gate. It is also important to strengthen and grow the capacity of those channels so that when you do work with the energy points, you can handle the results.

Rather than discuss the power points of the body in a single list of seven, nine, four, or however many chakras, I talk about them in terms of importance and how central they are to the work of sex magic.

Centers on the Central Channel

The Core Center

"The core center" is my name for what is known in China as the Lower DanTien, in Japan as the Hara, and in Hinduism as the seat of the Kundalini. It is roughly equated with the navel chakra or Svadisthana. It is the center of gravity in the body, and is about four finger-widths below the navel and a couple inches in front of the spine. This is the point that is the primary focus of most internal martial arts and is the seat of the original sexual energy we are born with.

A seat of immense power, it is also a seat of intense passion. If the energy in this center is cultivated at the expense of other centers it runs the risk of causing many emotional and at times physical difficulties, but it is nevertheless the primary point of concentration in much of sex sorcery in the East and West.

The Heart Center

The heart center is the seat of the higher emotions and the center of the astral and soul bodies. It is the middle DanTien of the Chinese systems and the Anahata Chakra of the Indian systems. It is the point of fusion between the vital and atavistic powers that emanate from the core center and the purifying and ennobling powers that descend from the crown center.

Because it is the meeting place of the highest and lowest, this center gets a lot of attention in mysticism. The union of god and man that can occur simply by meditating on this point is sometimes represented in Christian mysticism by the heart with an eye at the center.

The Crown Center

The crown center is the Upper DanTien of the Chinese systems and the Sahasrara Chakra of the Indian systems. It is here that the seed of divine wisdom and bliss resides. When one fully activates, abides in, and operates from this place, one is a true Ipsissimus or Great Adept.

The core center is the root of the physical/etheric bodies, the heart is the root of the astral/soul bodies, and the crown is the root of the mind/causal bodies. By meditating upon and entering into each of these centers, we can shift awareness from one body to another.

The Root Center

This center is located at the perineum and is the same as the Muladhara Chakra in Indian systems. It is in control of drawing up energy from below through the legs and integrating it into the channels in the torso. This point is very important for grounding and centering and also for controlling energy released in sex.

Solar Plexus Center

Located under the heart center and above the core center, this center is known as the Manipura Chakra in India, and is a psychic gateway in the body. It is through this point that the astral body is tethered to the physical and etheric bodies, and it is also through this point that some psychics and magicians find it easiest to access the subtle body of another.

Energy from the core center gets balanced and distributed at this point, and in some ways it acts as an intermediary between the core and heart centers, just as the heart itself does between the root and crown centers.

Throat Center

The throat center or Vissudya is associated with expression and manifestation. It is a point where the descending influences of the divine can be released through and made material through the power of vibration. This is why spells that are spoken work better than those that are only thought: the act of vibrating them into the world gives them power to manifest. Being the point between the head and body space makes it a sort of canal between higher and lower worlds. This point is also integral to dream work, dreams being the speech of the subconscious mind.

The Star Center

The star center actually hovers above the physical body and the crown center. It is transpersonal and is in some ways a regulated gateway between you and the infinite. It plays an important part in collecting energy from outer planets and stars, acting almost like a computer to program such energies before they hit the body.

The Earth Center

The earth center does the same thing as the star center, but from below, and actually exists beneath the feet. Though I spoke of the central channel as extending from the perineum to the crown, there is a very subtle astral extension of this channel that travels between the legs and into the ground.

Centers Connected to Other Channels

The Third Eye

I know many of you were expecting me to list this earlier, as it is one of the classical seven chakras—the Ajna. It is not, however, directly on the straight line from root to crown; it is positioned further forward. Some systems connect it to the central channel by a separate channel, and others curve the central channel over and down at the top of the head to terminate in the third eye. I suggest the former is correct, but it is a subtle body after all.

Whatever the most correct description of its location, this center facilitates the higher aspects of sight and clairvoyance. It is connected to the physical eyes, and sometimes sex sorcery will create visions or even pressure at this place.

The Temples

There are power centers at the temples that help facilitate perception and internal balance. They are connected to the Third Eye; in fact, these three points form a triangle of perception that can be treated as a sort of internal scrying mirror with certain practices. Further connections from this triangle to the throat chakra or Jade Pillow at the back of the head create tetrahedral structures that are important in some advanced practices.

Rear Channel Points

There are several power points along the back channel of the body, very close to the skin:

☆ The sacrum relates to sexual energy and is integral to orgasm reversal.

☆ The spine across from the navel, known as the "door of life" in Chinese medicine, is one of the main places where the rear channel intersects with the belt channel.

☆ Mid-spine, near the T-11 vertebrae, is the entrance into the heart for healing purposes and emotional balance

☆ The skull base, also called the Jade Pillow and Mouth of God, is a center that is closely connected with the crown and throat centers and is said to produce a divine nectar that can be tasted by some yogis. It is also the place where you can connect to the logos within you and the place where true words of power can form before being uttered.

Front Channel Points

Points in the front of the body include:

☆ The genitals typically have three points: the testes or ovaries and along the shaft of the penis or on the clitoris. These form a triangle of manifestation. The intersection of these triangles is an important feature in some tantric symbolism.

☆ The navel is the point at which you were first attached to the external world. This is sometimes called the "Mind Palace" in Taoism. It is also where most energy exercises begin in Taoism, as opposed to various tantric exercises that begin at the core, crown, or root.

☆ The low heart point is at the bottom of the breast plate.

☆ The high heart point is at the top of the breast plate.

Hand Centers

In the palm of the hand is one of the most useful collection/release points for energy. The point is basically in the center of the triangle created by the three pads on the palm. There are other, smaller points at the tips of the fingers and in the cavity between the thumb and hand. This last point seems to link to a channel right into the brain and is a great tool in influencing magic as well as curing headaches.

Feet Centers

On the bottoms of the feet are a point that the Chinese call the bubbling springs. It is right behind the front pad. This is the major collection point for energy from the earth.

The Drops

The last part of the subtle body that I want to talk about are the drops or Bindus. These two drops are the red and white seeds that tantric systems claim you inherit from your mother and father. They get equated very closely to the Red and White Dragon in some Western alchemical texts.

The red drop is inherited from the mother. It is spoken of as red because of the color of menstrual blood, but is more properly thought of as the etheric equivalent of vaginal fluid. It is the seat of vitality and sits in the navel, or in some systems in the root chakra. The white drop is inherited from the father and is considered white to represent the seminal fluid. It is the seat of wisdom and abides in the crown.

The union of the red and white drops is one of the key features of inner heat yogas such as Kundalini and Chandali. Experiencing the bliss created by the experience in sexual sorcery leads one to spiritual advancement and gnosis, psychic power, and radiant health. The physical combination of fluids is a mirror of this union and, done skillfully, becomes the Elixir of Life itself.

Pulsing the Web

Though we have been focusing on a few main channels or subtle nerves, there are actually tens of thousands of them throughout, around, and extending from our etheric body. Energy is moving through them at all times, but a full and detailed map of these would take up several books this size and is not necessary for our work. What we need to do is to become aware of them enough that you can feel them, send energy into your limbs and various points in the body, and extend yourself outward when needed. This is a book on sex magic, so the work of sending energy beyond yourself is important.

The best introductory practice I know for getting a feel for the fullness of the subtle body is something I call Pulsing the Web. I perform this exercise many times a day. It can be done anywhere at any time.

STEP 1: The first step is to find your consciousness in the central channel, and move it up and down that channel in link with the breath. Do not pull in extra energy. Do not reject the extra energy that travels there naturally because of your attention. Just inhale and send your consciousness up the central channel to the crown of your head. Exhale and send your consciousness to the root center at the perineum.

STEP 2: Inhale and send your consciousness to the crown of the central channel, but now send it down and up the front, rear, left, and right channels as well. You should feel your energy/awareness moving down all four channels in unison and gathering at the base. Do not circulate energy up one and down another. Pulse up and down with the breath.

STEP 3: Inhale and center yourself in the heart center. As you exhale send your energy and awareness outward, up and down the central channel, through the other four main channels, and out the four limbs. Contract again as you inhale. Note the feelings and sensations, as well as any changes in mind state.

STEP 4: Perform the same pulse as Step 3, but this time seek the extremities and channels that branch off from the main channels we have worked with thus far. Feel your awareness move out into the fingers and toes. Feel it branch out from the central channel into the eyes, ears, medula, temples, and so on. Feel how smaller subtle nerves connect from the main channels to the power centers and organs. Take special note of any that draw your attention in a special way as these may be key to undoing a blockage or establishing some special ability in the future. If you have the time, you can draw a map of these channels.

STEP 5: Perform the same pulse as Step 4 and extend it beyond the physical body. Move above the head into the star center. Feel for the channel that descends from the central channel down into the earth like a vestigial tail. Feel for the channels that move beyond the hands into the ether. Feel for the belt channel that surrounds you like a spiral and acts as your natural shield. Contract back again. Note how some of these, such as the belt channel and tail channel, are quite solid in comparison to the more subtle channels that extend from the hand and hair.

STEP 6: Move even further and further out in terms of both physical space and etheric subtlety. At what point are you moving into things that are "not you"? How does this affect your sense of self? Can you pick up impressions from the web that surrounds other objects and people? Do you extend into other dimensions or planes, and do you shift naturally simply by moving your attention?

Practice this casually throughout your day; no one even needs to know that you are doing it. It will greatly assist you when you start performing sex magic with another person.

CHAPTER 4

The Dragon's Breath:
Breathing Techniques and the Inner Fire Practice

This chapter will present exercises in breathing and the all-important Inner Fire. Most of the magic contained in this book depends upon establishing competency in the Inner Fire technique. It is the key to the alchemical transformation of sexual energy into spiritual energy, and the transformation of the sexual fluids into the Elixir of Life. This is the most important chapter in the book. Even if you do not ever practice any of the sexual sorcery techniques in the rest of the book, you can gain immense benefit just by practicing what is in this chapter.

Some people confuse competency with mastery and perfection. By *competency* I mean the ability to perform these exercises without strain on the body, or strained attention. You will be having sex while doing some of them, so if you are overly worried about breathing correctly or visualizing channels a particular way it will disturb your attention for the other aspects of magic, as well as your focus on the sex itself. *Mastery,* on the other hand, comes from performing the practices throughout years. *Perfection* is the work of a lifetime. You should not worry about mastery or perfection in order to move on, but you do need to establish competency.

Every Breath You Take

Before we can really master any kind of sex sorcery we need to master the breath. There is a reason that in many cultures the word for *spirit* or *energy* is also the word for *breath*. In Hebrew the word is *ruach*; in Tibetan it's *lung*; in Sanskrit it's *prana*; in Greek it's *pneuma*; in Arabic it's *ruh*. Even the word *spirit* or *spiritus* itself means "breath" in Latin. The breath *is* life, yet we pay surprisingly little attention to it. It is the only part of the autonomous nervous system of which we can take conscious control, and thus it is the first step in grabbing the reins of the aspects of body and mind that rule over *us* rather than the other way around.

In terms of sex sorcery the breath is what will bring body, energy, and mind together to act as one entity in harmony. The body needs to be managed so that orgasm occurs at an optimal moment—this is regulated by the breath. The mind will need to be focused on either a desired outcome or resting in clarity instead of simply embroiled in baser sexual thought—the breath will bring the mind into focus while still allowing performance and ecstasy. Most importantly the energy of the orgasm will need to be steered towards a particular goal, recirculated in the body for health, or toward particular points in the body that will lead to higher states of awareness—the breath is what redirects and drives this. The breath is the one key that unlocks 100 practices.

Preliminaries

We need to establish a few preliminaries. The first is that none of these techniques should be practiced on a full stomach. It is not necessary to fast or perform them with no food at all in your stomach, but you should eat light and wait an hour or so after eating.

Second is that they must be learned with the back upright and vertical. You can sit in a chair or on a cushion, but you should not learn them lying down, leaning back, or slouched. The reason is that you will be learning to gather and manipulate energy in the central channel, and any leaning one way or the other will affect the movement of that energy. Eventually you will be using some of these breaths in different sexual positions, but unless you first learn to do them with the spine straight and vertical, you will not be able to manage the feat while laying down on a bed, kneeling, or in any other pose.

Lastly, you should, whenever time allows, perform the nine purification breaths to cleanse the breath of impurity before each session. If you do not have time you can skip it, *as long as you have been doing it on a regular basis*. If you have not been doing the nine breaths and other purification exercises it is essential that you do it before each session.

Unless otherwise noted, *all* breaths, both inhaling and exhaling, are taken through the nose, not the mouth.

The Vase Breath

The first breath we need to cover is called the Vase Breath because you are filling the lungs the way you would fill a vase with water: from the bottom up. It is the basis upon which all the other breaths will rest, so learn it well.

Your lungs will hold about seven pints of air, yet we generally only draw in one pint at a time. We also tend to favor the upper chambers of the lungs, puffing out our chests and holding in our stomachs. This may be a more physically attractive way of breathing, but it's not very efficient at oxygenating blood, regulating stress, reducing blood pressure, or calming the mind.

To perform the Vase Breath, you must make sure that your back is reasonably straight and vertical. Seated or standing doesn't matter, but do not do it lying down. Simply breathe in through the nostrils, keeping the mouth closed and filling the lower chambers of the lungs first. Allow the abdomen to distend as you do this. Then allow the upper chambers of the lungs to fill almost all the way. You should aim to take in about six pints of air. If you do this correctly your breath rate should slow from about 15 times per minute to about 8 times per minute.

Letting the abdomen expand is key. When learning it can be useful to place your hands in a point-down triangle over your lower abdomen so that the thumbs meet over your navel and your index fingers come together just above your groin. If you are doing it correctly the hands will separate.

In Kung Fu they teach that this breath should have the four qualities of *man, shen, xi,* and *jun*: slow, deep, fine, and even. When the Vase Breath is used, the blood and brain get a better flow of oxygen, which has many benefits. One of the primary benefits is that the pituitary gland begins to function optimally. This gland not only controls all the other glands in the body, but is also the physical manifestation of the Third Eye and the seat of mystical vision. If you are sensitive to the energies of the body you will also note the increased flow of vital force in the body as well as an improved ability to direct these energies using only the breath and the will.

You can and should practice Vase Breathing as much as you are able. On a cushion, in the temple, in the car, at the office—wherever you can remember to do it. Ideally you can actually make this your ordinary style of breath, but that takes much practice.

The Locks

Once you have the Vase Breath down you should learn to apply locks that will help stop energy loss, increase intensity, and cultivate the Inner Fire and power that you will draw on in your sex sorcery.

The Root Lock

The first lock you must master is the root lock, called the Mula Banda in yoga. This lock will enable you to stop the release of bodily energy through the lower gates, reverse the flow of orgasmic energy, and, in men, stop the release of fluid during orgasm. Use the following steps:

1. To perform the root lock you need to perform the Vase Breath while contracting the anus and pelvic floor. You can identify the correct muscles for this by stopping and starting the urine stream while peeing. *Note: Do this during urination* only *to find the correct muscles. Doing this exercise regularly while emptying your bladder can actually weaken the muscle.*

2. Hold the contraction for five seconds, five times in a row. Work your way up to 10 seconds, 10 times in a row. Take care not to flex other muscles while learning to employ the lock.

3. Release the lock and feel the flow of bodily energy rise upward as a result of the release. It takes time to strengthen a muscle you have had very little cause to exercise before, so be patient. Eventually the lock will be strong enough to hold for long periods of time, and in men will be strong enough to stop the flow of semen during orgasm.

The Upper Lock

The upper lock, sometimes called the chin lock, throat lock, or Jalandhara Banda, is used to cap off the upper gates. Similar to the root lock it stops the release of bodily energy. This also reverses the flow of upwardly moving energy in the body, and when employed with the root lock it creates a sort of hydraulic pressure that cultivates the Inner Fire.

1. Take a Vase Breath and focus on the throat. At the end of the inhale swallow a little spittle and hold your throat closed. Roll your shoulders slightly forward and tuck

your chin. Some teachers of mind claim that the swallowing and chin movement are only there to teach how to apply pressure from above but are not strictly necessary. Others claim that they are necessary. Personally I follow these instructions.

2. Hold the contraction for five seconds, five times in a row. Work your way up to 10 seconds, 10 times in a row

3. Raise the chin and let the air out slowly, steadily, and evenly—not in one exhalation. Feel how this cultivates a rise of energy slowly up the central channel into the head.

Once you have mastered the upper lock on its own you can employ it simultaneously with the root lock. Note how the downward flowing energy moves upward, and the upward-flowing energy moves down, gathering in the base of the vase—your lower abdomen. We will do more with this later.

The Middle Lock

The middle lock or diaphragm lock is called the Uddiyana Banda. This lock encourages movement in the central channel, massages the organs, and further stimulates the pressure that is created by the root and upper locks.

1. Take a Vase Breath and *exhale. Note: The other two blocks are learned during inhalation—do not attempt to learn this during an inhalation.*

2. Draw the abdomen inward and upward as deeply as you can. This can involve rolling the shoulders forward and stretching the back slightly.

3. Hold as long as you can without experiencing discomfort.

4. Inhale with another Vase Breath.

To further assist in this it is sometimes useful to roll the shoulders forward and bend slightly. Once you have gained competency in this technique you can employ it along with the root and upper locks on an exhale. This will cultivate a feeling of upward motion in the body that will be essential in the work of the Inner Fire.

Bringing it All Together

Before we add in visualizations and energy manipulation you should get used to using all the locks together in succession. A routine should look like this:

1. Inhale a Vase Breath, filling the lower chambers of the lungs and expanding the abdomen.

2. When you have drawn in almost as much as you can, perform the root and upper locks. You can also draw the stomach in slightly to increase the pressure in the belly.

3. When you cannot take it anymore take a short sniff of air, then slowly exhale.

4. As you exhale, bring the lower abdomen in so that it feels like you are almost scooping the breath up from the bottom of the belly. Exhale until *almost* all the breath has been expelled. You should feel an upward motion of energy in the body, almost as if you are releasing a pressure valve.

5. Upon the exhalation employ all three locks: bring the anus and pelvic floor up with the root lock, bring the chin and throat closed with the upper lock, and bring the abdomen up and in with the middle lock. Doing these locks at the end of the exhale allows the movement of energy to continue even after the breath has been taken.

6. Begin again with step 1 of this process and repeat as necessary.

The Vase Breath and the three locks are the main breath system that I would like you to master for the main exercises needed to cultivate the Inner Fire.

The Inner Fire

If you can perform the Vase Breath and locks process you are on your way to being able to stoke the Inner Fire. In Tibetan it is called Tummo; in Sanskrit it is called Chandali and Kundalini. Sometimes people think physical heat is the actual point of the process because people have been able to raise their body temperature with it in order to thrive in cold climates.[1] But actually the physical heat produced is a side effect, not the point itself. The point of inner heat yoga is a process of sublimation in the subtle body that creates clarity and generates bliss. This blissful clarity, as well as the increased functioning of the subtle channels, is the point of this practice, but it is also the basis for many sexual magical practices. It is a process of alchemic *sublimation*—literally making yourself more sublime.

As with the parts of the subtle body, there are numerous traditions and innovations on the precise details, yet some key points exist in all methods. For instance, the Second Dalai Lama, when explaining Niguma's system, provides two different visualizations in the same text! The method I am explaining here is very simple and does not require any culturally specific visualizations such as Tibetan or Sanskrit letters. It is also presented in stages so that your first sessions can focus on the core essentials, and then further stages can incorporate other elements.

Step 1: Body as Luminous, Empty, and Divine

You must visualize your body as being made of light. It is divine, and luminous, and perfect. Like a balloon it is empty inside, save for the chakras, channels, and drops that we spoke about in the last chapter.

In Chapter 6 I will talk about taking on god-forms and generating divine pride; all that has its roots here. In Tibetan Tantra you would see yourself in the form of your meditational deity, which you would have practiced for a considerable amount of time in what is called the "Generation Stage." Because this is *not* tantra, but rather a technique borrowed from tantra, we can see ourselves in an idealized divine version of ourselves, or as a god or goddess with whom we are working closely. More on that later. The important part is that the body be empty like a balloon other than the channels and chakras.

There are many reasons we do this, but primary among them is that it keeps the increased energy of sexual sorcery in line with our best aspirations. As I stated in Chapter 2, increased energy in the body means increased emotions, and, unless we are purified, this can mean increased anger, ignorance, and delusion.

Step 2: The Drops

At the base of the central channel you should see a red drop. It's very small—the size of a mustard seed—and radiant in power. At the crown of the head you should see a white drop, also the size of a mustard seed, and also radiant. In addition to this there are dimmer white drops at the throat, heart, and navel. All of them are very small. You do not have to visualize the chakras in any particular manner for this exercise. Visualizing wheels with channels extending out of them through the body is good enough. Different texts will emphasize different channel counts of "lotus petals," but for now, just keep the visualization loose.

Place your mind at your navel chakra. This should not be mere attention paid to the navel as though you are looking at your belly button. You should feel as if you are inside your central channel looking up at the heart, throat, and head. Throughout this exercise, your main focus will be at the navel. Even when triggering action elsewhere in the body, you are doing it from the position of the navel.

Take a deep Vase Breath and perform the lower and upper locks. When you do the lower lock, see the red drop shoot up from the testes or ovaries at the root of the central channel to the navel chakra, which is located about four finger widths beneath the belly button, and about three inches in from the spine. Hold the locks on inhale for as long as is comfortable. *Note: I said* comfortable, *not as long as you can. You are not trying to strain yourself.*

Step 3: Visualization of the Fire

When the red drop raises from the sex center and strikes the navel center it stokes a fire when it hits. Visualize it as blazing hot and radiant. Do not lose the sense of luminosity and divinity as you hold it.

As you exhale, let the air out slowly, as if you are releasing a pressure valve. See the fire rise through the central channel. As you exhale, perform the lower, middle, and upper locks and hold for as long as is comfortable.

Breathe in again and feel the energy enter through the nostrils down into the central channel, stoking the fire that is blazing there, making it glow hotter and brighter. Again exhale. Repeat this process for as long as time and comfort allow.

Step 4: Dripping and Blazing

Eventually you will feel a strong presence at the heart, as if the heat from the navel is now consuming it. Let the fire circulate around the heart chakra three times. Visualize the dim white drops at the heart melt and drip down into the fire at the navel. This causes bliss to descend over you as the white drop melts. When it hits the navel it pops like butter on a fire and adds bliss to the fire, which now blazes even hotter and higher.

Continue with the Vase Breathing and locks and allow the fire to raise to the throat. Let the fire circulate three times. The same thing happens to the white drop there. It descends, bringing bliss, and increasing the flame.

Finally the flames reach the crown. Let the fire spin at the top and let the great white seed there melt and descend. Now a great bliss—a mahasukha, descends over the whole body and the fire consumes all. You may feel or even visualize the white and red drops merging at different places in the body. If your attention is still focused on the navel it will likely happen there. You can at this point raise your attention to your heart and let the drops merge there if you like. Doing it at the navel will increase bliss and heat, which is better for sex sorcery, but merging at the heart is better for creating meditative stabilization and non-dual awareness. Merging in the throat is done to help facilitate dream sorcery, but I would urge you to only attempt it after you are very comfortable with merging at the navel and heart. Merging at the head is a no-no unless you are under the direct supervision of someone who has done it.

At this point it is helpful to place the tip of the tongue to the top of the mouth. This connects an important channel for the downward flow of wisdom nectar. Taoists will be familiar with placing the tongue to the roof of the mouth behind the teeth from Microcosmic Orbit practice, but in this practice it is best if you can roll the tongue back as far as is comfortable and touch on or closer to the soft pallet. This is called the Kechari Mudra in yoga, and it helps cultivate the nectar's descent.

Step 5: Expanding Outward

At this point you can let the fire and bliss fill the body, overflowing from the central channel and into the side channels and out into the cells of the body. Let the fire even leave the eyes and nose and flow out into the hosts of deities or beings around you. Let the world be aflame with bliss and clarity.

Effects and Dangers of Inner Fire

It is *essential* that you approach the practice of Inner Fire with gentleness, patience, and care. Very real damage can be done to the physical body when working with the etheric body. Some effects people have reported include:

☆ Pressure behind the eyes, in the throat, or at elsewhere along the central channel.

☆ Heart palpitations.

☆ Temporary loss of sight—or astral sight so strong that it eclipses ordinary vision.

☆ Increased depression, anger, or other negative emotions.

☆ Stomach pains and digestive troubles.

In all these cases the problems can be solved by being gentler in your practice, circulating the fire at the various problem points, being patient with some temporary effects, keeping a solid meditation practice, and, if necessary, doubling down on purification practices.

Bellows Breath

The Bellows Breath is a way to increase energy in just a few seconds. I can use it instead of coffee in the morning if I have to—I have used it a lot at 3 a.m. when writing chapters of this very book. The technique is simple. Take a full, deep inhalation, than exhale rapid, short, sharp, forced bursts. You should be able to exhale about 30 short breaths in 10 seconds. After about three breaths like this, switch back to the Vase Breath. As you inhale, focus on drawing the breath deep down, toward the genitals. As you exhale, move your focus up the spine to the top of the head. The vital force will follow your mind. After a few breaths in this manner, you can go back to the short, sharp, rapid exhales.

The rush that this breath technique provides is tangible and acts as a sort of reboot for the brain. Some people have even used it to fend off cravings for cigarettes and coffee.

Doing the Bellows Breath just before beginning Inner Fire meditation, and interspersed within the Inner Fire process, is a great way to increase the potency of the fire.

Reverse Breath

The Reverse Breath is a technique used by Taoists, alchemists, and martial artists to gather and pack energy into muscle tissue, bones, and the energy body—specifically the belt channel that surrounds the body like a spiral and provides natural shielding.

Reverse Breathing gets its name from the motion of the abdomen: rather than expand the abdomen with the in-breath, you draw it in; rather than draw in the abdomen with the out-breath, you expand it out. Other than that you still want to perform the breathing as you would the Vase Breath: fill the lower chambers of the lungs first, followed by the upper chambers. Here are the steps of the Reverse Breath:

1. Take a deep inhalation, and as you do draw the abdomen inward and upward while doing the root lock, clenching the anus and perineum.
2. Exhale and push the abdomen out, releasing the lower lock.
3. Feel how the energy of the breath, rather than staying in the central channel as with the normal Vase Breath and locks, gets distributed and "packed" into the body.

People who often feel tired, have little libido, or simply want to cultivate good health should consider doing some short sessions of reverse breathing at the end of meditation or yoga sessions to redistribute and pack energy in the body. It should not, however, become a normal mode of breathing, and people who have not mastered the normal Vase Breath should avoid it entirely. If you begin to Reverse Breathe as your normal method of breathing it can cause health problems associated with lack of oxygen.

Doing the Reverse Breath after a session of Inner Fire will help distribute the energy evenly throughout the body, leading to greater health and dispelling any lingering feelings of threshold sickness, or not being able to return to "normal" awareness and functioning.

Embryonic Breath

The Embryonic Breath is not really something that you can *do* as much as it is something that *happens*. Many people who meditate or do relaxation exercises have noted that they seem to just stop breathing, yet not run out of breath. In reality the breath has not stopped but has become so shallow that the lungs are no longer moving discernibly and the normal movement of the chest and abdomen have stopped. This can happen to many people about 10 minutes into a post-coital meditation session, thus my mentioning it here in the context of sex magic prep.

Although you cannot willfully force yourself to breathe this way, you *can* keep the phenomena in mind and not let it disrupt your meditation or freak you out when it happens. It is actually a very good sign to have this happen, but many people become disturbed when it registers that they have not been breathing in a normal way. When this happens, just carry on. If it feels natural to abide in the state of Embryonic Breathing, do so without fear. If it feels natural to resume normal breath, then do that and don't worry about losing some precious attainment. Just abide in the state and be natural.

Basic Breath Meditation

Some of you who know my works well might be surprised that I have not discussed meditation yet. Normally I push meditation as the cornerstone practice upon which everything else rests. Certainly meditation is important in sex sorcery, but in this work it actually takes a backseat to the Inner Fire in importance. It may seem strange to place basic meditation instructions at the end of this chapter rather than the beginning, but in this case it is a supportive practice to other work. In other words, if you only have 20 minutes to spare in your day, and you are serious about performing sex sorcery, use it for Inner Fire. With practice you can integrate it with meditation anyway.

That said, a regular meditation practice should always be part of your life. If you can, you should meditate a bit every morning and evening—15 to 20 minutes for each session is great. Linking the two sessions together with small five- to 10-minute sessions when you have the opportunity will help increase your success and blend your natural clarity with your ordinary living levels of awareness. I meditate in parking lots, in bathrooms, in parks—wherever I can get a moment to myself.

A regular meditation practice will better enable you to hold the object of the sorcery in your mind while you are having sex. It will enable you to handle the sometimes strange and unbalancing experiences that can result from Inner Fire. It will allow you to release what needs to be released, and keep attention where you need it. More than this, it will help you destroy your monkey mind and dwell in the bliss/emptiness that is created by sex sorcery.

To begin meditation, sit in a chair or on a cushion or in your favorite asana[2] with your back straight. Begin your session with the nine purification breaths, releasing all tension and thoughts of the past, present, and future. Following that, breathe slowly and naturally, and relax.

Focus your attention on your breathing. Don't stalk it like a cat stalks a mouse. Enter into it. Flow in and out with it. The past is a memory. The future is a projection. The present disappears before it can be grasped. Just allow the mind to be gently aware of the breath. Relax completely during the inhale and exhale. Let thoughts arise and fall away with no attachment.

If you are like most people you will find that distractions arise nearly instantly. Once you recognize that you have left the meditation and are distracted with a train of thought, you should simply return to the breath without chastising or criticizing yourself. In fact, you should have no expectation whatsoever about how well your meditation goes. Lust of result is the biggest obstacle to meditation. Recognize that thoughts emanate from nothing and dissipate into nothing. Rest in the breath and in primordial awareness.

In all likelihood you will at first spend most of your meditation session doing little but being distracted, recognizing it, and returning to the breath, only to be distracted again. Many of my students who find themselves in this situation claim that they can't meditate, and they give up. What they don't realize is that they *are* meditating. They are training their minds to recognize when it is not acting according to their will, and bringing it back from distraction.

I meet people all the time who claim to be bad at meditation. Many even claim that they can't meditate. They tell me that they tried in the past and couldn't "get there" or "clear their minds." They would like to meditate, but they just suck at it. I have good news: **You cannot be bad at meditation.** Barring serious mental illness, everyone can meditate.

The problem can be summed up as *expectation* and *tenacity*. The expectation of what is supposed to occur in meditation is often a lot grander than what actually happens. People expect that they will sit down, the mind will quickly quiet, and it will stay perfectly still for the length of the session. They will feel a calming peace they have never felt before and be at one with everything. These expectations are unrealistic, especially when the subject is willing to give all of three sessions' worth of effort toward the goal before declaring that he or she *cannot meditate*. This lack of tenacity is even worse than the unrealistic expectation.

The first thing to do when undertaking meditation is to abandon any lust of result. You should *expect* to be distracted almost constantly. In fact, if you are keeping a regular practice of meditating every day, you should expect nothing but distraction for almost six months! You sit and focus on breath, or mantra, or object, or whatever, and a thought of food arises in the mindstream. You start thinking about dinner. Which gets you thinking about the time, and how much time as passed so far. You realize that you have lost focus...

This is the crucial moment. When you recognize that you are distracted, the natural reaction is to berate yourself because you stopped meditating. The secret is this: *You did not stop meditating.* You recognized your distraction; that *is* meditation. If you can then return to the focus without judgment you will continue to meditate properly. If you willingly continue to be distracted, knowing that you are distracted, *now* you have stopped meditating.

Some distractions are more insidious than others. A problem for magicians, witches, and psychics is that distractions often arise in the form of visions. If you are meditating and trying to experience the real nature of mind that is beyond subject and object, then even visions of your patron god or goddess need to be set aside as distractions. This is the meaning of the Buddhist axiom, "If you see a Buddha on the road, then kill him."

If you spend your whole life experiencing nothing in your meditation sessions other than being distracted and returning to the focus of the meditation, you will have accomplished quite a lot. You will master your own thought process. I cannot stress enough what a wonderful feat this is. Almost everything people do, say, and think is just a mechanical reaction. How you were raised, what you ate for breakfast, what traffic was like, what genes you inherited, how you are dressed—these all impact every moment and push us one way or the other. If you can recognize the mind being distracted by habitual pattern in meditation, you will learn to recognize these patterns in the heat of everyday life. The next time someone pushes your buttons and you start to react, you will probably catch yourself and be able to react from a place of real thought rather than habit, because you know how to recognize attachment and distraction. Good job!

Of course, most people *will* eventually experience more than just this process during the course of their meditative journey. You may see visions, you may feel bliss, you may feel the barriers of the self melt away. All of this is what Tibetans call Nyams, which I translate as: weird shit that happens during meditation. None of it is as important as the process of recognizing distraction. Eventually, with practice, you will probably experience some genuine subtle states described in classical texts such as Rigpa or Samadhi, but these come with time, and must not be sought after directly. Even if you do not experience these states, you will have accomplished much just by taking a little bit of control over your own mind.

CHAPTER 5

Flying Solo:
The Sorcery of Celibacy and Masturbation

We are all sexual beings, and as such, sex is impacting us at all times, whether we are having it with someone else or not. The moment you decide to make sex a part of your spiritual and magical practice is the moment you have decided to take charge of your sexuality, and thus you need to have a strategy for how to channel sexual energy. This not only comes from sex itself, but also from sexual urges and stimuli.

Supernormal Stimuli

Nobel Laureate Nikolaas Tinbergen found that in the animal kingdom, if you could find key factors that animal instincts focused on, you could present the animals with a *supernormal* stimulus that would make them reject normal behavior in favor of the exaggerated version. Songbirds would abandon their own pale blue eggs so that they could sit on black eggs with fluorescent polka dots that were so big the birds would fall off constantly. Songbird parents would feed fake baby birds whose mouths were open wider than their own real chicks. The songbird chicks would ignore their own parents in favor of seeing food from fake birds with more dramatic markings.

This idea of supernormal stimuli is important to keep in mind, as it is something we are faced with every day. In the past people have dealt with seeing attractive people here and there, but if they wanted to seek sexually explicit stimuli, they would have to go out of their way to find it. Today the situation is very different. Various media confront us not only with sexual imagery but extreme imagery at every turn. In line at the grocery store we are confronted with images of sex. While watching TV, we are confronted with images of sex. While out doing just about anything, we are bombarded with sex stimuli. While writing these very words, I have the capacity to instantly summon up any type of pornographic material that I could possibly desire with just a mouse click. This has an impact on the psyche that we are only just beginning to understand.

Please don't get the impression that I am anti-pornography or some kind of Puritan who wants to purge media of sexual images—I am not. I think we can all enjoy the pleasures of hyper-stimuli if we remain aware of what is going on. I am only saying that, given the unprecedented level of stimuli we take in, we would be fools to think it has no effect on us. Indeed, studies are consistently showing quite the opposite: people who watch excessive amounts of pornography can wind up losing interest in their mates, or people who focus on a particular kink or fetish lose the ability to become aroused during sex that does not involve that fetish.

As sexual sorcerer you need to be aware of the stimuli you take in and monitor how it affects your life. Are you being fed with the kinds of sexual stimuli you choose or what is chosen for you? Are you losing interest in the "real" in favor of fascination with the hyper-real? Are you in command of your sexuality, or is it in command of you? It is not a matter of pure or impure, right or wrong, or good or bad. It is a matter of whether you are the master or the servant. The sexual sorcerer is the master of his or her sexuality.

Abstinence and Celibacy

Before we get into sexual practices, even ones we do on our own, we should take a look at abstinence as a type of sexual sorcery all its own. Abstaining from sex can be done for specific periods of time such as when on retreat or preparing for a particular magical operation, or it can be a vow of celibacy that is intended to last a lifetime. In either case it is a conscious attempt to create change in the mind/body/world through controlling sexuality, and so it belongs in this book.

Celibacy is recommended by many spiritual leaders and religious paths. Some leaders, like Gandhi, clearly have a negative view of sex in general, calling life without celibacy "insipid and animal-like." Others, like Sivananda, had a more balanced view. He said, "It is beyond all doubt that the life of a Bramhacharya [yogic celibacy] is glorious and marvelous. At the same time, a life of moderation in the household life is equally good and helpful. Both have their own advantages. You must have great strength to tread the path either way."

As much as I respect Gandhi's political accomplishments, he clearly had issues about sex. In the 1920s and '40s he sent squads of followers to destroy erotic representations in temples across India, especially representations of gay and lesbian erotic acts. If we are to choose celibacy for life or for a temporary vow, let it be out of its own benefits rather than out of hatred of sex itself.

The benefits people report from celibacy are numerous. First there are psychological benefits: you begin to see yourself as someone who is worthy beyond the concepts of beauty and desirability. I once had a conversation with a young Catholic Nun in Philadelphia. I was in my early 20s and I think I made a sort of offhand joke that it was a shame she was a nun because she was so pretty. She thanked me, and told me that celibacy was actually the greatest gift to her because until she decided to give up sex, she saw herself as, and was treated largely as a sex object. Far from a shame, celibacy freed her to become a much more whole person. Not only does celibacy free you from thinking of yourself as a sex object, but it frees you from thinking of other people that way as well. It allows you to see people in your life as who they really are, not merely for their appearance and what pleasure they might provide.

There is also the idea that when freed from emotional attachment to one single person, you are now free to give yourself to the world and have a more balanced life. This is one of the reasons behind celibacy for monks and nuns of both Buddhist and Christian faiths. Their compassion is meant to be aimed at everyone, equally, not merely toward a circle of family and friends.

Many people who take on celibacy as a spiritual or magical discipline report physical changes as well: increased physical strength, improved memory, better skin, hair regrowth, waves of warm and cool bliss, and even a more pleasant bodily odor. All these results have been shared with me by those on the path, and thus are anecdotal, but they are in keeping with the results promised by various traditions.

The main magical benefit of celibacy is increased energy. Many schools associate the loss of sexual fluids with the loss of energy. In certain tantras like Kalachakra and in Taoist alchemy, the type of energy lost during sex is a type that is irreplaceable. This generative chi or prana diminishes over time and contributes to aging, weakness of health, mental instability, and overall lack of wellness.

Some types of celibacy practice increase energy not only through retaining generative force you would otherwise lose, but also through increasing overall energy in the body by alchemically transforming sexual energy into spiritual vigor. This is a way of preparing an internal elixir of life: melding the male and the female energies already inside us to produce a state of wisdom, bliss, and health.

You have already been taught one method of doing this in the last chapter on breath and inner heat where the red and white drops merge. To add the dimension of sexual input in it all you have to do is first meditate on sex itself. Some visualize themselves in a sex act, which is what is recommended in many Buddhist tantras, and others simply take the sexual energy they accumulate throughout the day, which, as I have already noted, is there in overabundance, and integrate it into their channels. Keith Dowman said in his book *Sky Dancer*, "Strip the [tantric] yoga of its arcane terminology and there is a simple meditation technique: stimulate the desire and then use it as the object of meditation and it becomes awareness—a field of Emptiness and pure Pleasure."

Taoists do this practice of marrying the male and female energies already present in the body as well and call it "Single Cultivation" because it cultivates both essences from the same subtle body. A key difference in technique is that they focus on moving energy in what is called a "Microcosmic Orbit" rather than gathering the force at the crown. This allows the energy to circulate around the body, which produces a less drastic and much gentler experience than the Inner Fire method I showed in the last chapter. I will discuss this method further when I talk about cultivation of the orgasm.

Apart from the simple avoidance of sex there are also those who attempt to be chaste in thought as well, seeking to avoid as much sexual input as they can. Even if this is not the level of dedication you plan on maintaining through your life, it is wise at the beginning stages of a vow of chastity to avoid sexually explicit material as much as possible. Learning new things to keep the mind busy, ignoring the comments of those who do not understand or support the decision, and in general keeping away from any activity that you find sexually exciting for a few weeks at the beginning of a vow are essential to getting a good start. After a few weeks to a month most people feel a dissipation of stronger urges and are better able to socialize, enjoy media, and resume their normal life without a constant temptation.

Apart from those who decide to practice celibacy as a lifestyle are those who might abstain from sex before embarking on some major magical project. Many of the grimoires recommend periods of abstaining from sex as part of the purification exercises that precede angelic or demonic summoning, but most of this has to do with Christian ideas of purity. For those of us who engage in sexual magic, it can be helpful to undergo periods of abstinence in order to build up generative force and sexual desire.

At the very least, even if there is no specific period of abstinence, the sexual magician should learn to not squander his or her power. The moment that you decide sex is sacred and a tool of sorcery, it does not do to simply masturbate to pornography or have sex with people you do not value. A sorcerer keeps his or her magical tools clean, sacred, and ready to use in the art.

Masturbatory Magic

We come now to masturbation as a magical practice. Given all the talk about losing seed and generative force in the preceding discussion on celibacy you might think that I consider it to be an entirely fruitless or even dangerous dalliance. I do not. It has its drawbacks, but it also has its pleasures and benefits. Applied skillfully as part of a strategy it can be a very useful pursuit, and is in fact necessary for training in certain methods before you attempt them with a partner.

Just as celibacy has benefits, so too does masturbation. Masturbation lowers blood pressure and produces endorphins that ease stress and aid relaxation and sleep. In men it can help cleanse the urinary tract and reduce infections. A 2003 study from Australia found that because of the removal of toxins from the urinary tract, men who ejaculate five times a week have been found to be a third less likely to develop prostate cancer.[1]

Masturbation can also aid men and women in maintaining the muscles used in sex. During periods of inactivity with a partner it can be useful to masturbate in order to exercise the pelvic floor muscles, which will help keep both men and women in performance shape, as well as help prevent incontinence as you get older.

Lastly, it's simply just pleasurable. Masturbating releases dopamine and oxytocin, which lift spirits, boost happiness, and make you feel good. Outside of taking drugs it is the single biggest blast of dopamine available. Although it certainly can diminish sex drive if done too frequently and in conjunction with supernormal stimuli, in moderation there is no reason not to enjoy it for the sake of enjoyment.

The Sigil Spell

There is a method of casting a spell that has become so famous and ubiquitous that I almost don't want to include it here because it has been written about so much elsewhere. Basically, you create a sigil to represent something you wish to accomplish and then make sure that you are looking at that sigil while you have an orgasm—usually, but not always, through masturbation. The idea is that at the moment of orgasm a lot of energy is released and can be used for sorcery. This relates to the tantric idea that the orgasm is close to a primordial experience, and thus taps into the underlying nature of reality. The act is seen to create a magical "child" or to "give birth" to your intention.

The method gained popularity in Chaos Magic circles in the 1980s and '90s, and gained true fame when the comic book writer Grant Morrison asked his readers to participate in a "Wank-a-thon." His groundbreaking series *The Invisibles* was in danger of cancellation so he placed a sigil in the letters column of the comic and asked readers to masturbate over the sigil while looking at it. The sigil worked and the comic was renewed, but there was so much excess energy that he credits it with landing him in the hospital.

The method is simple enough and has only two main parts that you need to be concerned with: The sigil creation, and the generation of an orgasm. It's worth saying a few words on both of these.

When it comes to creating sigils there are numerous methods you can employ. You can use a premade sigil from a magical text, such as a sigil of Venus to bring love or perhaps the Tibetan letter Dzam to bring wealth.[2] You can also trace a sigil on a kamea (or magic square) or Rose Cross using the letters that encapsulate your desire. Planetary kameas can be found in Agrippa's *Three Books of Occult Philosophy*, and the Rose Cross is a Golden Dawn tool found in several books, but you can also generate your own kamea for the purpose. To do this, simply draw out a 5-inch by 5-inch graph containing 25 boxes and place each letter of the alphabet (a–z), in a box as inspiration and spirit dictates. Of course, our alphabet has 26 letters, so you can either let I and J be in the same box, or omit the C and use K or S to stand in for it depending on the sound.

A few years ago, following an invocation of the god Aeon, I came up with the following arrangement that has served me well. If we use this chart to draw our intent, let's say the word LOVER, we can have something like this:

B	S	E	X	Q
R	D	K	M	F
T	I	A	O	Z
V	H	O	C	G
N	W	U	Y	P

Probably the most popular method of creating sigils is attributed to Austin Osman Spare, even though it was written about centuries before him and used in books ranging from Agrippa's *Occult Philosophy* to the Enchiridion of Pope Leo. It basically consists of writing a sentence of your desire, crossing out repeating letters, and then binding the letters together into a sigil. So for instance the phrase "double my profits this month" might look like the figure on the next page:

The method I prefer, and the one I use in my own practice, is to try to scry, feel out, or otherwise receive a glyph directly. This could be something received from a deity in response to a request, similar to the 16 Jupiter Glyphs I used in my book *Financial Sorcery*, or it could be generated by your own artistic genius and ability to graphically represent the power you wish to embody. The sigil on the cover of this book is an example of a sigil received in this manner. It was invoked by me to be a probability binding seal, but was received and drawn by Matthew Brownlee, the sorcerer-artist who does most of my illustrations.

This type of sigil is, for me, much more potent than a jumble of letters. When invoked by someone with a genuine connection and reified by a talented artist, there is an anima to this sort of sigil that is lacking in more contrived methods. Secrets that can be read in the lines, arcana in the angles.

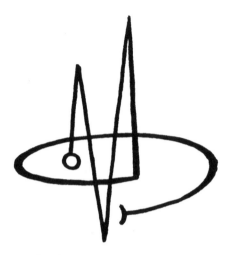

Whatever the method you use to generate the sigil, the second part of the equation is the orgasm itself. This sigil method can be used by two people having sex together and is in fact a bit easier and more powerful that way, but for now we will restrict the discussion to masturbatory methods.

The trick to much of sex sorcery is maintaining passion for sexual activity while also maintaining focus on the magic. If you are used to using pornography for masturbation you can place the sigil around a computer monitor or other image so that you can shift focus back and forth as needed. If you prefer to close your eyes and engage in a sexual fantasy, it is beneficial if the fantasy can somehow relate to the object of the spell. It need not be directly involved, but could be just slightly related. For instance, imagine a new promotion lands the perfect man as your office mate, or perhaps an affair with your secretary. In the case of Grant Morrison's *Invisibles* Wank-a-thon, I chose to fantasize about one of the main characters in the book. That's right: not only am I writing about it, I participated in it.

Andrieh Vitimus, in his book *Hands-On Chaos Magic*, notes that the quality of the orgasm has much to do with the strength of the result, and that simply masturbating in the same manner you do regularly, especially if you do it several times a week, will likely not generate much force. Those making a serious attempt at this practice might want to abstain for a week or so before the operation in order to build generative force and lead to a more potent orgasm.

Having materials or fantasy chosen ahead of time as well as other temple accoutrements set up also helps. For example, there is no reason, during a martial-style ritual, not to have five red candles, or red sheets, or any other symbolism associated with Mars or the arts of war. One sorceress I know uses vibrators for this purpose that are strapped in place so that her hands can remain free to place in a series of mudras she has developed to aid manifestation. Bullet vibrators in a condom could probably be used by men with similar effect.

I will also add that doing the Inner Fire practice before your session and maintaining at least the vase breathing during the actual masturbation will also yield a much greater result in terms of orgasmic potency. You will need to really have the whole process internalized, but with time this should not be a problem.

After the rite is done, many Chaos magicians advise you to forget the whole rite so that it has a chance to make its way into the subconscious and do its thing. I find this to be a kind of "training wheels" approach to magic. After some basic training and experimentation your mind should be more than able to see and remember the sigil without it effecting the result. In fact, some sorcerers, such as Gordon White, the proprietor of Rune Soup,[3] recommend leaving the sigils out where they can be seen. There is much more to be said on the subject of sigil magic, and Gordon's blog is probably the very best place to start. Gordon, more than anyone I can think of, has been taking the art into the new century with his methods of sigil shoaling, scalability, and targeting.

We will revisit the idea of sigils and sex sorcery later in the book, but for now there is one further aspect of masturbatory magic we need to discuss.

Fluid Retention

I mentioned in the chapter on breath and inner fire that mastery of the lower lock, the lifting of the pelvic floor that happens when you tighten the anus and perineum, can be used by men to block semen loss during orgasm. This is a practice that certainly can and should be used during sex with a partner, but it can be difficult to achieve without practice. It is *much* easier to master this technique when masturbating. There are two main reasons for this: First is that when you are masturbating you can control the speed and pressure of the stimulation. If you find yourself unable to perform the lock and hold it, you can ease off and keep at it until you are ready. You also can shift body position, even adopting a classical asana, without having to worry about a partner. The second reason is that if you have not mastered the lock completely, you can use the three-finger method to retain the fluid. To do this simply reach down to the lower gate at the perineum and block it with the index, middle, and ring finger. This will block the semen similar to how the lock would. One or two fingers can block the urethra, but often fluid will escape. The three-finger method is a traditional Taoist method of cultivating chi and blocks all but the smallest amount of fluid that remains in the tube.

There is another cheat that is used in India: Sit in Siddhasana or what is sometimes called "half lotus." In this position you have one leg drawn up and in as far as you can with your heel under your perineum. The other leg sits in front of the inner leg with the foot drawn up on the opposite thigh or just left on the floor. The key here is the heel blocking the perineum, which will have the same effect as the three-finger technique.

In both of these techniques you will likely lose your erection after your orgasm just as you would if you came normally. If you can manage to retain semen using only the locks, the breath, and your willpower, you can often maintain your erection through one or more full-body orgasms. This is the secret of male multi-orgasms.

Most of the fluid will be reabsorbed into the body and converted into other substances. Testosterone especially will be saved and re-circulated, which for older men is especially vitalizing. On the ethe-ric level the vital force gets transformed into vital essences—Chi in Taosim, Tejas and Ojas in Indian tantras. The specific names and such are not that important.

The energy from the orgasm will flow upward and result in a very pleasurable, but different type of orgasm. The first time I ever experienced this I exclaimed, "Wow—it's like plugging your dick into your brain!" That remains a pretty good description. It results in a sort of full-body orgasm that may not be as instantaneously gratifying as orgasm with seminal release at first, but with time and practice it can become a much more satisfying, enjoyable, and healthy experience.

If you perform the Inner Fire technique before and after this type of orgasm, the melting bliss that you experience in that rite is multiplied a hundredfold, and truly opens a gate to experienc-ing the highest states of non-dual awareness. You are not far from having the mind of a Buddha. Being an Ipsissimus is not far off. The state can be accessed, at least temporarily, through the orgasm that shakes the whole body, unites the male and female drops, and sim-ulates the ego-shattering state that some Western magicians call being beyond the abyss, and what others might call enlightenment.

With semen retention you will be able to hold this state of mind and enjoy the bliss of orgasm much longer than with a traditional orgasm, but you will still eventually come down. The ego will re-assert itself, and things will return to normal—almost. The more you practice, the more powerfully each cosmic-bliss experience will reverberate in your normal mind-state. The more you retain genera-tive force, the stronger, healthier, and clearer you will become.

Though the bulk of this section has been aimed at men, women can also practice the lower lock and Inner Fire during orgasm. There is no semen to retain, but your vital essences that escape through the lower gate will still be blocked and flow upward. Much of the work of the man is simply about accomplishing things that women do naturally, or can at least accomplish with less effort.

We will revisit this topic later in the book, but for now it is important to know that before you practice semen retention and force reversal with a partner, it is easier, and for some people *vital*, to master it during masturbation first.

CHAPTER 6

When Gods Get it On:
Invocation, God-Forms, and Sex

In this chapter we will begin our exploration of sexual sorcery between two people, and what better way to start than by discussing union between two divine beings. My favorite quote on this type of work is from the Chandamaharosana Tantra:

Therefore, one who desires Enlightenment
Should practice what is to be practiced.
To renounce the sense objects
Is to torture oneself by asceticism—don't do it!
When you see form, look!
Similarly, listen to sounds,
Inhale scents,
Taste delicious flavors,
Feel textures.

Use the objects of the five senses—
You will quickly attain supreme Enlightenment
The man [sees] the woman as a goddess
The woman [sees] the man as a god.
By joining the diamond scepter and lotus,
They should make offerings to each other.
There is no worship apart from this.

Sounds great, right? Through invocation, adoration, meditation, and other means you focus on divine nature. By then engaging in the bliss and the ego-shattering orgasm of sexual sorcery you get to experience the reality of that nature.

In this chapter I want to focus on two main methods to accomplish this. The first is taking on the nature of an already established god, goddess, or spirit from a specific tradition and performing *as* that being. The second method focuses on resting in your own innate divine nature and experiencing it without the aid of a contrived deity from a specific religion or tradition. The former is more accessible but the latter is, in my opinion, more beneficial. We shall start with a discussion of specific deities entering into union.

Gods and Goddesses

Magicians invoke deities into themselves all the time in order to embody certain qualities, attain knowledge, establish spiritual authority, or attempt to reveal their own divine nature by interfacing with the god or goddess in question. By having sex as these beings sorcerers loosen their hold on their own ego and can actually experience the sensation of *being* this divine being.

Through inviting gods to partake in such an intimate and carnal act, we also give the gods a foothold to manifest in our physical reality. This is part of what the classical Hieros Gamos, Greek for "Holy Marriage," were about. In Sumeria, the King of a city-state would engage in sex with a sacred prostitute. He would be Dumuzid and she would represent Inanna. Their union would bring the blessings of love, fertility, victory in war, and all other blessings of Inanna to the state as a whole. In Greece the union of Zeus and Hera in a similar fashion was said to be celebrated at the Temple of Hera at Samos. There is some evidence to show that the union of Demeter and Iasion was also celebrated in such a fashion in order to promote fertile crops.

More recently the Great Rite of Wicca transmits the blessings of the god and goddess to the coven in more or less the same way. The High Priest and Priestess unite as the god and goddess opening the pathways for them to experience divinity, and for the gods to enjoy corporeality. The blessing they receive is in turn passed on to the coven in the form of wine and cakes consecrated by the couple.

Beyond worship and manifesting of divinity and blessings there is another benefit to invoking and then merging with a god or goddess: by doing so the sorcerer is able to undercut the lower, more base passions of sex for sex's sake and focus on the magical work at hand, be it spiritual ascension or sorcerous effect. This idea of transcending carnal pleasure is one that is stressed in much of the writing on sex magic in the West. Paschal Beverly Randolph, for instance, wrote:

> *The union of the man with the woman must be innocent. Lust for pleasure must not be the main purpose. Transcending carnal pleasure, aim at the union of the spirits, if you want your prayer to be exhausted by ecstasy. If you conform to these principles the sexual act will become a fountainhead of wisdom, happiness, and peace.*[1]

Although I think it goes a little far to suggest that sex magic must be "innocent" or utterly free from lust and pleasure, his point about not simply engaging in ordinary sex is well made. If we are to hold the mind of a god or goddess during this rite, it can only aid in keeping the act sacred.

Traditional Pairings of Gods

The first question you have to address when embarking on this work is, whom do you invoke into yourself and your partner, and why?

If you are from a tradition where this practice is established it is an easy choice. All Higher Tantric Deities in Tibetan Buddhism have sex-yogas connected with them, so you would take on the pairing described in the tantras. Even in some outer tantras deities that are usually practiced alone can get paired in Yab-Yum for different effects. For instance, the Drikung Kagyu have a practice in which you visualize yourself as Red Dzambhala, a wealth god, in union with Kurukulla, a goddess of enchantment, passion, and attraction. The Nyingma have a practice of Manjushri, a Bodhisattva connected with intellect, in sexual union with Saraswati, goddess of wisdom and the arts. Similarly you can focus on gods who are traditionally married such as Jupiter and Juno, Odin and Freya, and so on.

Just be careful, as some god and goddess pairings in mythology do not end well. Although Aphrodite and Ares make a very hot couple of love and war, their union was an extra-marital affair that caused a fair amount of drama. Innanna and Dumuzid are a traditional pairing for this exact type work, but let's not forget that she sold him out to Ereshkigal's demons so he could take her place in the underworld. People forget that Innana is not and never was a goddess of marriage.

LGBT Gods

When I was researching this book and talking with some LGBT friends, one practitioner of tantra suggested that even gay couples should seek out male and female deity pairs for sex magic because of the polarity expressed. This certainly is an option, especially for couples in which one person feels that he runs feminine energy despite being born male, or in which she runs male energy despite being genetically female. From what I have experienced most gods have very little trouble with being invoked into a person of the opposite gender.

That said, there are also plenty of homosexual pairings and bisexual deities. Horus and Set are the first ones to come to mind as beings who have had sexual relations in myth. They represent opposite sides of a polarity and have been traditionally linked in many magical texts, from ancient Egypt to modern Typhonian Thelemic works. Odin likewise has been connected with some activity with Loki that some see as homoerotic, and he also took the unique step among male Aesir of studying the feminine Vanir Mysteries from Freya. Astarte, Artemis, Helen, and Labrys all have connection to lesbian mysteries. I myself have seen a Tibetan Thanka of Tara in union with Tara, but could not get a straight answer on what practice it might be connected with.

Whereas many transgendered people will simply invoke a deity of whichever gender they most closely identify with, there are a few transgendered deities, as well as some who have played at being the opposite sex. Aphroditus, the so-called bearded Aphrodite, comes to mind. Hir holy name, Hermaphroditus, is from where we get the word *hermaphrodite*.

Agdistis is another example, albeit a tragic one, as hir androgyny was seen as a threat by other gods. Dionysus slipped Agdistis a sleeping potion and tied hir ankle to hir penis. When s/he stood, s/he castrated hirself, and the blood fertilized the earth, giving rise to the first almond tree.

You can find gay, lesbian, and transgendered gods and mythologies throughout the world, but you should in no way feel constrained to such beings. The gods are much larger than that. If couples of any orientation want to invoke hetero, homo, or transgendered pairs in their rites, they should express themselves in terms of sexuality and divinity however they wish.

Nontraditional Pairings

In today's Wild Wild West of eclectic Paganism people are experimenting with pantheons they know almost nothing about and

criss-crossing other pantheons in ways that are sometimes staggeringly ill-conceived. Just a few years ago I was contacted by someone who was putting together a Samhain rite for her coven. Their
High Priestess wanted to call upon Ghede and Santissima Muerte
as "The God and Goddess" in the ritual because they were both concerned with death (fair enough) and the coven wanted to work in
the "African" Pantheon. This person wanted to know if I had any
advice. I explained that neither was from Africa. Ghede was from
Haiti and his female counterpart, if you absolutely *had* to work that
way, would be Manman Brigitte, not Santissima Muerte, who is
from Mexico and is quasi-Catholic. The only advice I had in this situation was to ask the priestess to step down and disband the coven
before someone gets hurt.

Of course there is nothing inherently wrong with an eclectic approach to practice, it just has to be done with intelligence, respect,
and a bit of research. As Peter Carroll recently stated in his new
book *Epoch*, "All Gods and all religions and all magical traditions
get cobbled together out of the bits of previous traditions. All theol-
ogy and all revelations look suspiciously like syncretism, and schol-
arship confirms this." Far from an invitation to just go crazy and
do whatever you like, this idea should be treated as a challenge to
research, seek initiation where appropriate, experiment, and move
forward based on good results.

Some elders claim that you will be fine as long as you stick within the same pantheon, but I strongly disagree. For example, whereas Aphrodite does not *know* Thor because they are from different
pantheons, she absolutely *hates* Helios because he told her husband
Hephaestus about her affair with Ares. She in turn made Helios fall
in love with a Persian princess named Lukothoe. Aphrodite then
warned her father of the affair so that he would put her to death,
thus breaking Helios's heart. World religion is full of stories like
this, and whereas the pantheons may well be the archetypes of different noble virtues, they are also the archetypes of dysfunctional
families.

So what do you do? How do you choose if you are not sticking
to a tradition? Well, before you go ahead and choose to invoke Kali
into yourself and Jesus[2] into your husband, it is good to see if they

work together well in a nonsexual dual invocation. I mean, it's tense enough introducing friends to other friends for coffee; you would not expect them to have sex immediately, right?

In all cases a pattern of research, experimentation, research guided by results of experiment, and further experimentation is key. You should also incorporate divination into the process. Basically, be smart, be respectful, and pay attention. If you decide to do a sex magic rite in which two divine beings are uniting, and all hell breaks loose in your lives shortly thereafter, poor research might be the reason why.

Monotheistic Pairing

Many practitioners are Christians or Jews and thus are not keen on calling Pagan gods into themselves. There is plenty of room here for work to be done, though. Christians can focus on the uniting of Sophia and Christ Logos, and both Jews and Christians can focus on the union of God and Shekhina. In both scenarios the feminine is separated from the Father because of sin and the fall of man. The sexual union is the reuniting of both God and his bride, as well as God and mankind.

Though many people will take the descriptions in the Song of Songs, the Pistis Sophia, and the Kabbalah as purely symbolic, there is evidence here of actual sexual practice: "Their desire, both his and hers, was to unite Shekinah. He focused on Tiphereth, and his wife on Malkuth. His union was to join Shekinah; she focused correspondingly on being Shekinah and uniting with her husband, Tiphereth."[3]

In the Gospel of Philip, the bridal chamber is listed as one of the mysteries and sacraments: "The Lord did everything in a mystery, a baptism and a chrism and a eucharist and a redemption and a bridal chamber."

The gospel goes on to speak of the bridal chamber in less than clear terms, but suffice it to say that many believe it was a sacred sex act or Heiros Gamos that was practiced in the very early days of Christianity. Others, including many modern Gnostics, argue that

it is symbolic. This book is not the place to make a definitive schol-
arly argument one way or the other; I will simply state that people
have interpreted it this way, have practiced based upon this interpretation, and have claimed to receive Gnosis thereby.

How to Invoke

Once you have chosen a being to invoke, you need to call upon
that being. There are numerous methods for this, and numerous
results you can attain. The results depend not just on method, but
on your personal gifts and the relationship you have to a particular
deity as well. I have experienced pretty much the full gamut over the
years, ranging from a light sense of the deity's presence that is only
maintained through strong concentration, to full-blown possession
such that I cannot remember exactly what happened after the invocation and had some difficulty coming back fully into myself. Most
of the time, though, it is somewhere between the extremes.

As to a method, I use a four-step method that usually generates
a strong presence, sets aside personal ego for the moment, and does
not easily yield itself to full possession, which is not necessarily desirable and is not the goal of the practices presented in this book.

Step 1: Close your eyes and visualize your own body dissipating
into space or light. Spend a moment with a clear and clean mind
and a sense of non-self. This setting-aside of the self is not going
to completely remove your consciousness, but merely lessen your
attachment to your own ego. This making room is not something
that should be lingered on for a long period of time; like trying not
to think of elephants, the more you attempt to set the self aside, the
more it asserts itself. It is best to simply see it dissipate, and then
move quickly to the next part, instead of sitting in silence trying to
be empty. Nothing could be more contrived and counterproductive.

Step 2: Reemerge as the deity in question. If the deity in question is connected to a seal or symbol I will first imagine that symbol
arising as a seed from the emptiness. The symbol then radiates light
in all directions and reflects back upon the source, taking the shape
of the god or goddess in question. If you simply wish to visualize

that deity arising from emptiness or have some other process that stimulates the generation, that is all fine. The idea here is to use your imagination and will to create a "body" that is resonant with the characteristics of the deity. You can think of this as a throne into which the presence of the being can pour its essence and take shape. Or, if you like, as providing a hospitable environment for an alien presence to inhabit.

As an addendum to Step 2 you can decorate the temple and wear a costume that is also appropriate to the situation. A Statue of Venus, green tapestries to make the walls of the temple, seven candles, and so on might assist the presence of Venus. Wearing clothing appropriate to the deity or bearing his or her implements is likewise appropriate. This sort of thing is very useful in group ceremonies in which a large number of people all need to be on the same page, but is less vital when it is just you and a partner. That said, sex rituals that begin with a god undressing another god are kind of sexy and not a bad way to stir the passions while maintaining the sacredness of the rite.

Step 3: Call out to the deity in question. This is usually done as hymns of praise recalling the qualities, powers, and great deeds followed by an entreaty to come and merge with you and be present at the rite. For example:

Oh Mother of Love, Oh maiden of beauty
Daughter of tides and Keeper of Mirrors
You who bends the hearts of gods and men
Places desire in the minds of lovers
And stirs passions in even the coldest of souls
You who is loveliness itself
And who is surrounded by legions of nymphs
Ascend naked from the sea
Descend glorious from the Star of Morning
Ride forth gently on the breeze
Fill my soul with your presence

Enflame my heart with love and life
Move my body with the madness of your lust
Come. Come.

In this invocation we have a movement from the third-person perspective, in which we are simply talking about Aphrodite in the first two lines, to the second-person for the rest of the invocation, in which we are actually addressing Aphrodite directly. In lines 3 through 7 we are simply reciting lines of praise that serve to please the deity, tune our own minds to that "vibe," and fine-tune the purpose of the invocation. Note that all the references are to love and passion, not to Aphrodite's propensity for vengeance, jealousy, or in some cases domination. Invocations referencing those qualities and deeds would highlight those qualities in her presence. Lines 8 through 13 are an invitation for her to pour herself into you. As with the rest of the invocation it is peppered with references to her history and symbolism.

In this step you open yourself to the presence of the deity. This is should not be a complicated act. Simply clear the mind and allow the presence to take residence. If you have been meditating and doing inner fire practice this will be *much* easier than if you are not. Both of those practices have a way of attacking ego clinging, enabling to set yourself aside.

One thing that you do have to be careful of here is expectation. Some people get to this stage and expect to hear a voice directly, or even to be fully ridden or "possessed," as it is sometimes called. Those things *can* happen, but not usually. Furthermore, it is not really desirable for your own consciousness to be set aside completely. The point of invocation in this context is to meld your being with that of the deity, not to go somewhere else while a deity controls you. Sometimes you feel nothing at first, and the deity asserts itself during Step 4.

Step 4: Move from second-person into first-person and assert yourself as the deity. This can be done as further lines in the invocation, or as getting up and simply asserting yourself to be the deity.

If we were to attach lines to take our Aphrodite Invocation to Step 4, we could add:

I am Nepher'ri, the Beautiful Eye!
Philomeides, the lover of laughter
Epistrophia, who turns always to love
Unite with me and lose yourself
In the Love of Heaven
And the Throes of Passion
Be Mine!

Here the lines again refer to her history, symbolism, and traditions. The Egyptian[4] and Greek names further serve to cement her presence, as they are from the languages she was traditionally connected with, and thus spoken for the first time by her rather than by you. She then issues an action for what she has come to do, in this case unite with someone in a rite of sexual magic, but it could also be to simply bestow blessings, enchant lovers, protect a sea voyage, or whatever.

A lesson I learned while doing invocations publically is, whether you feel the presence at first or not, get up and act it out anyway. In other words, fake it 'til you make it! The first time this ever happened to me was during an invocation of Horus I performed in front of a mixed crowd of about 30 people at a Unitarian Church. I felt a slight presence, but nothing earth-shattering. I got up and addressed the crowd as Horus anyway, and started going around blessing people. I really don't know at what point it started to not be me, but the last thing I clearly remember is feeling my physical face change into a hawk's head and anointing someone's head with oil. After that I anointed about 25 more people and gave individual messages to some. My own consciousness started to reassert itself during the closing ceremonies, which were performed by an assistant.

The point is that the presence was not triggered directly by the words or the ritual, but by acting as the deity itself. This is why in

Vodou some of the possessions occur during dances sacred to that Loa, or why in tantra the connection is strengthened while repeating the mantra of the deity. Don't try to "make" it happen, instead just "let" it happen.

The Higher Method

An alternative to invoking a traditional god, goddess, or spirit into you is to simply see yourself as divine, and your partner as divine. Acknowledge the divine, the Buddha Nature, or the Logos within you, and which *is* you.

Those whose religion and practice are focused on worshiping a god or gods who are external to themselves may question why I call this the Higher Method. In today's occult landscape, which is kind of obsessed with turning to spirits and gods for intercession and blessing in every endeavor, it is easy to forget that we *are* spirits. We *are* divine. There is nothing to invoke, nothing to obtain; you have this nature already. According to one way of thinking, the best an external deity can do for you is help you realize it and unlock it, but you do not *need* them to do so. You can do it on your own. It is a simpler and more subtle technique than an invocation, but if done with full conviction it can lead to even greater heights and provide an easier path to the deepest levels of occult initiation and spiritual realization.

The exact methods for doing this can vary. In my Strategic Sorcery course I teach a method for generating several specific divine bodies for this purpose. In this book, however, I shall focus on simply utilizing the universal centering rite gesture to generate a sense of inner divinity, then dwelling in that state.

The universal centering is as much of a meditation as it is a gesture. Its simplicity and ease of practice should not take away from its power. It is a very quick and efficient method of unlocking your own divine nature and putting you into a position of spiritual power and authority. It is as powerful as any invocation at doing so.

Universal Centering Rite

Sit or stand with your back straight. Make a fist with your left hand and place it over your heart. Cover it with your right hand and apply about 5 pounds of pressure to bring the vital energies of the body into the central channel near the heart. Perform the Vase Breath and consider your heart to be the very center of your being. Close your eyes and consider that your heart is the very center of the universe. Do not imagine that you are somewhere else, but that you, in the room where you are, are the center around which all creation revolves.

Just as our perception that the sun revolves around the earth is destroyed by taking a larger perspective from space, consider that, from the ultimate perspective, the whole cosmos revolves around the seed of spirit in the heart. Do not think that you are fooling yourself in this. You are in fact revealing a spiritual, if not cosmological truth.

With practice, you might feel the heart center vibrate with life—the physical manifestation of the awakened Logos. Consider that your body is luminous and divine, and your heart center is the center of everything. Drop your hands but continue in that state.

(The Rending of Space is also a useful gesture to employ at this time and tends to reinforce the realization of godhood or enlightenment. You can find the description in the appendix of this book.)

Uniting

The union of two divine beings is a moment of cosmic joy and creation. The invocation, meditation, and everything that came before it may be potent, but it is merely a setup to the union that truly opens the gate to the experience of the primordial nature of the divine. The tantras refer to two stages that I think can apply in many other traditions as well. The two stages are called Kye Rim, or Generation Stage, and Dzog Rim, or Completion Stage.

The Generation Stage is where all the outer ritual happens. The temple is set up, offerings are made, you visualize yourself as the deity, you say or sing praises, you invite the deity, and you even act as the deity by saying mantras or doing other actions. It's everything that is done to *generate* the experience. Completion Stage is where the results of the Generation Stage get actualized by working with forces in the mind and body that are tangible and cannot be mistaken for fantasy or wishful thinking. These can involve the winds and channels, sex practice, dream yoga, or other types of actions that may differ from practice to practice. In our case we will be working with sex and the moment of orgasm, which is pretty clearly a primordial experience that won't leave you wondering, *Was it all in my head?* In later chapters we will be incorporating more work with the channels and drops, as well as the physical fluids produced during sex. For now our primary focus must be on the act itself.

The trick to all successful sex sorcery is to uphold passion while also maintaining the sense of being divine. Especially for men, it is not the easiest thing in the world to maintain an erection if you are thinking constantly about your energy body and thinking of yourself as a divine being. The method that I find works best is to begin the rite with your own invocation and merging with the deity. Spend the first few moments of contact with your partner holding this in the mind, but upon beginning sex play you should shift to focus primarily on seeing the *other* person as divine, and allowing them to see you that way as well.

This focus on the other places your attraction and passion where it should be for good sex: on your partner. By treating him or her as a God or Goddess, by seeing him or her as a perfected being, you should have no trouble holding your passion. The attention from the other person will do all the work to reinforce your invocation— and actually, in my experience, reinforces it better than anything you could do in your own mind.

The sexual position you choose to use for this rite is up to you. Some traditional yogas recommend a couple adopt the Yab-Yum position, in which the male sits in lotus or Siddhasana and the woman sits on his lap. This allows both of your backs to remain straight, which helps cultivate Inner Fire and also allows for better meditation because you can have sex while remaining relatively still if the woman milks the penis using the lower lock or kegel exercises. Despite these advantages, I find that this makes the whole affair rather tame and sterile. Many other positions are possible, and really there should be no restriction. You can consult a book from the Kama Shastra for ideas, or you can just adore each other and let divine passion be your guide. In the next chapter, on sexual energy work, we will discuss some specific positions and techniques, but for this chapter I wanted to focus solely on the magical act of two divine beings uniting sexually and walking together through the primordial gate that is the orgasm.

The Orgasm and the Ego

The moment of orgasm is not just a sexual climax, but a magical one as well. In this moment the personal ego shatters and the mind enters a state that is beyond duality. It is this reason that the orgasm is called "La petite mort," or "the little death." This moment is like a gateway that the consciousness can enter and dwell in for a time. It is here that duality falls away, that self and other dissipates, and a primordial, luminescent awareness becomes our vantage point.

Sometimes when I start talking about the ego and transcendence people get a bit nervous, as though I am preaching an anti-life message, or saying that we should all seek to reabsorb ourselves in some ocean of oneness. That is not it at all. This is not a matter of destroying the ego, as many people seem to think. It is about transcending it. You still *have* an ego. Christ and Buddha and every other great master had an ego. It is about transcending it. It is about not being trapped in that ego. It is about plugging that ego into something universal and immense beyond imagination.

The example I always use in my teaching is to imagine that you are trapped in a cage on a desert island. Your first duty must be to break the lock and escape the cage. Once you do that, you are free to come and go, but you might find that the cage, now unlocked, is the best shelter on the island. The ego is like this cage: it can be a trap or a tool; it depends upon your ability to escape it. Slow paths of development might take lifetimes to accomplish what can be experienced within the space of one skillfully achieved orgasm.

The Strategic Orgasm

Most people would never consider approaching their orgasm with anything resembling a strategy. Unskilled people have sex, and, if they have an orgasm at all, it just comes when it comes. Of course, as sex sorcerers and sorceresses we have some options when it comes to that moment, and there is no one right way or wrong way to do it. Different approaches have different effects.

The first thing we need to know is that there are five stages to an orgasm. These hold true for men as well as women, though the time frames differ. They are:

1. Swelling; the engorgement of genital parts with blood
2. Contractions of muscles
3. Orgasm as psychosomatic event
4. Ejaculation of fluids
5. Deflation

The timeframe for women between stages three and four, if four happens at all,[5] is much longer than it is in men. In fact, the timeframe between orgasm and ejaculation in men is so short that most men consider them the same thing. They are not, and this is important for taking control of your sex life in general and performing quality sex magic specifically.

If you are both generating yourselves as deities it is ideal that you reach orgasm simultaneously. Unfortunately, there are barriers to this for both sexes. Men tend to reach it too quickly, and somewhere between 60 and 70 percent of women report not being able to reach orgasm at all from vaginal stimulation alone. For men the method is to cool down and pace yourself. When you feel those contractions start, back off and don't penetrate so deeply. Take deep Vase Breaths and practice at least the lower lock, if not all locks together. Have her squeeze the head of the penis with her vagina or pull down gently on your scrotum. If you keep using the locks, and willing the energy up the spine, it will fend off orgasm and allow you to last long enough to keep pace with your woman.

For women, the biggest obstacle is also the timing of the man's orgasm. Whatever you can do to assist your man in staving off climax until you are ready will go a long way to achieving simultaneous orgasm. This includes squeezing the head of the penis with your vaginal muscles, and reminding him verbally to slow down or place attention elsewhere. The other issue is that many women cannot reach orgasm through vaginal stimulation alone. The solution here is for the man to begin stimulating the female before himself, and, if necessary, for both the man and woman to do whatever they can to stimulate the clitoris with fingers during intercourse.

In all this an intimate knowledge of your partner also goes a long way toward accomplishing your goal—which is an argument some sex magicians use for keeping in monogamous, or at least non-promiscuous circles of partners.

Although not *essential* to sexual sorcery, there is a power in simultaneous orgasm that is hard to replicate any other way. If you cannot or choose not to strive for simultaneous orgasm, you can perform individual adorations of each other, such that, for a time, the god concerns himself with the adoration of the goddess and she concerns herself with nothing more than receiving pleasure, melding, and exploring the moment of orgasm as a divine gate. The roles can then reverse: the goddess adores the god and he absorbs his mind in pleasure.

Fluid Retention

The other strategic question that comes up about the orgasm is whether to release seed during the orgasm or retain it. You may think that this is only a question for the male, but it is not. Even though a female does not usually ejaculate outside the body, the etheric effects of using the locks and Vase Breath to close the lower gate and send the downward-flowing energy upward in the central channel still has many benefits. That said, it is a far more important question for the male, who often gets drained easily and is not as prone to multiple orgasms or stamina as the female is.

The key is that if you are a sex sorcerer you should be consciously choosing whether to release your seed for a purpose or whether to keep it and convert it into fuel. It is a matter of having sovereignty over your sexuality, and not yielding it even to your partner unless you choose to. I would argue that even those who do not buy into the promises of bliss and rejuvenation that come with semen retention should at least learn to do it so that they now have the control to choose when and how to release. Some argue that it is not only important for your benefit, but also for that of your partner.

David Deida wrote in *The Way of the Superior Man*, "One part of your woman is happy that she made you come. She is happy you are relaxed and enjoying yourself. Another part is disappointed that you've allowed yourself to choose a temporary and pleasurable spasm over the endless ravishment of her and her world."

The basic physical methods for stopping orgasm have already been described—using the locks and Vase Breath or the three-finger method. Your partner can also use the three-finger method to stop the seed, but even then it is you who must redirect it up the central channel. To simply leave it will eventually create an ache in the groin. If you use the breath and the will to direct it upwards, you experience a full-body orgasm that truly is just as enjoyable as releasing seed, and is also linked to greater bliss, spiritual and physical rejuvenation, increased confidence and awareness, and a host of other benefits.

Though we already have the basic knowledge of the method, to actually deploy it in the heat of passion is another matter. This is why the basics were covered in the chapter on masturbation—practice makes perfect, and you really need to have developed the muscles strongly in order to lift and hold the pelvic floor well enough. You should be practicing the lower lock and the Vase Breath several times a day, every day. Especially on a day when you plan on having sex.

During sex you should absorb yourself in your partner, worshipping his or her divine form with your own. Keep focus away from your own pleasure; let your partner take care of that. Be relaxed. Let yourself flow into your partner and your partner into you. Believe it or not, this getting lost in another actually lessens the need to release seed by shifting the focus away from every pleasurable sensation we have. A skilled sorcerer will not only flow into his partner's presence, but the divine presence that she has invoked. Flow through your partner into infinity.

If you have done the preliminary work you should start using the lower lock periodically during sex and increasing it as you get closer to climax. You should do it repeatedly a minute or so before you ejaculate so that when you do orgasm, it is an almost natural response. When the climax comes, if you can, deploy all three gates. If you cannot manage that, then at least lift the pelvic floor to stop the seed, and Vase breathe while *willing* the energy up the central channel. This will flow to the top of your head and radiate downward and out over the whole body. Abide in the sensation, as well as any colors or images that present themselves. Dwell in it with your partner. Feel the two become one.

In the next chapter we will discuss energetic techniques to take this to new levels, and the chapter after that we shall discuss practices that are focused on the physical fluids, not just the etheric substance and energy.

CHAPTER 7

Energy, Ecstasy, and Enchantment:
Working with Sex, Fire, and Mind

In the last chapter we dealt with the most basic level of sex magic practice, the uniting of two divine entities. In this chapter we will be introducing more complex techniques of manipulating energy and mind through sex. This will be done in addition to the work of invoking a deity or seeing ourselves as divine.

You might be thinking that it is too complex to really do during sex, but I assure you it is not. Simply gain competency in each technique to the point that you can do it without any trouble, and then move on to the next. This way doing the locks, etheric body work, or similar practices will come naturally and be *part* of sex play rather than something you are arduously trying to maintain while having sex. We gain competency from practicing each technique on its own. We gain mastery from employing the techniques together during real work. Perfection is the work of a lifetime.

Exploring and Flowing

The very first thing partners should do is explore each other fully, both physically and ethereally. A great way to begin this process is to stand or sit at opposite ends of the temple (the temple being wherever it is you are performing the rite) and perform the Inner Fire technique and then Pulsing the Web. You should now not only be full of energy, but also hyper-aware of your own channels and the ways in which they interact with the energetic patterns of everything they are in contact with.

Turn your attention now to your partner. Feel him or her across the room and feel his or her attention on you. You are already connected through the astral philotic lines, astral connections between all beings, and if you have had sex in the past, that connection is strong. Feel the component of this that is actual energy, not just an emotion you feel.

Move toward each other slowly until you feel each other enter the outer shell of the astral body. This usually happens somewhere between two and four feet from each other. Mentally give your partner permission to enter this space, and feel your channels mingle as you get closer. Take turns exploring just the astral body by moving your hands and face over your partner's body, about 6 inches away from his or her skin. Take note of feelings and impressions as you do this. You can sometimes feel the gates at this point—special points of entrance into the astral and etheric body. It is not only okay but recommended that you talk to one another during this process. Talk about points that feel pleasurable, that feel vulnerable, that feel stressed. Let your psychic impressions as an explorer be shared with the person being explored and listen to his or her feedback.

A fun experiment is to map these out on paper and then compare them to some Taoist and tantric maps of the subtle body and see where your map corresponds to tradition.

Move now to the physical body and again take turns exploring each other. You should not both explore at the same time. Let one person stand or lie still and be explored. Use your hands, mouth, tongue, to move over the body and know its contours. Obviously you will hit upon the primary sexual zones: the penis, vagina, breasts, and anus, but make sure that you do not spend all your time there. Pay special attention to the following areas:

☆ The crown of the head (the part that was soft when you were a baby)—this is where the consciousness is said to exit when you die, and where you want to direct your sexual energy to achieve higher states of consciousness

☆ The third eye

☆ The temples, important for balancing the solar male and lunar female energies in the body

☆ The areas around the physical eyes

☆ The throat, just above the breastplate—this is the seat of the throat chakra and the thyroid gland

☆ The medulla or jade pillow at the back of the head where the neck meets—this is the root of our most primal instincts and a place where spiritual nectar is said to be produced

☆ The soft spot under the collarbones

☆ The solar plexus

☆ The mons pubis

☆ The inner thighs

☆ The perineum—this area is exceptionally important, and as you can see has been getting a workout in our exercises thus far

☆ The coccyx

☆ Up and down the spine—see if you can feel out areas where there are said to be gates in Taoist models

☆ The bottoms of the feet—a lot of energy gets passed through the feet, and according to reflexology it affects the whole body

☆ The fingers and palms—there are many gateways and channel terminations in the hands that travel through the whole body (this is why magical gestures like mudras are so effective)

Once you are both done exploring the body in this fashion, try to send your mind into your partner. Flow in through his or her gates and see what you can sense. Mentally travel to your partner's heart chakra and see what you can sense. See what your partner senses when you are there. Travel around and get the lay of the land. Depending upon your psychic gifts this might be very rewarding or a complete waste of time.

Apart from the knowledge one gains of one's partner, this process can make for damn good foreplay. If you engage in sex after this, then all the better, but do try to refrain from ravishing each other until you have done the exercise.

Inner Fire and Sex

The Inner Fire meditation, Tummo in Tibetan, has been the subject of much interest and even university studies in which monks have been able to raise their body temperature up to 117 degrees in laboratory conditions. People dedicate their lives to the practice and master many physical exercises called Trul Khors that help cultivate that level of heat and bliss. A practitioner at this level may spend two to six hours a day working on this alone.

This level of dedication and training has caused some to question whether laypeople should even attempt it, and, if they do, when and how it should be done. Some Lamas reserve it for only advanced disciples. Other Lamas, such as those who have taught me, recommend it for just about everyone. At a recent teaching on Tummo, a student commented that he would not have the hours per day recommended by the Dalai Lama for mastering the practice. The Lama asked him if he was married, to which he answered yes. So the Lama told him to do it while he is having sex and to try to have sex at least three times a week. He noted that it was not optimal to *only* do it during that time, but if he only had a small amount of time per week, that would be the best time because the Inner Heat is intimately connected with sexual energy. He noted that several Westerners who practice it just at this time, and therefore are doing a less intense regimen than is sometimes taught, get amazing results that help reshape their mind, body, and world.

It is all too rare to hear Lamas speak with this amount of candor, and because I do not wish to get anyone upset I am withholding his name. The point he made, though, is an important one. Even the small sampling of techniques in this book may seem overwhelming to some, but if you focus on what you *can* do and don't compare it to people who do more, you can get amazing results. For instance, many people take a Kung Fu class once or twice a week. They get health benefits, they learn how to fight, they learn discipline, and they learn some of the internal energy work that helps keep them young and potent. The fact that they cannot run off to China and be Shaolin monks does not deter them, and it should not deter us.

The Inner Fire practice can be done before, during, and at the climax of sexual intercourse. Your first few times cultivating the fire while having sex are best done with both of you seated, with the female on the lap of the male, facing one another. Sex should have less thrusting and more internal motions such as moving the penis by lifting the pelvic muscles and milking the penis with the vagina. Lean into one another, and act as one.

If this feels different from when you perform the Inner Fire by yourself, it should. Every time you do the locks during sex you are not only pulling your own sexual energy up, but you are also drawing in a little bit of the sexual essence of your partner. When you combine your own white and red drops, the lunar/female and solar/male essences, respectively, during the solo Inner Fire process, there is still more of one energy than the other. But during the sex act, every time you perform the locks you draw a bit of the sexual essence of your partner into yourself, and this creates a near-perfect balance and a stronger inner alchemical result. In the next section we will show how to get even more out of this process, but for now, you should just get used to performing the Inner Fire during union without focusing specifically on drawing from the other person. It will happen naturally.

As the fire rises, you can talk about where in the body you feel it. If you feel it at the heart, keep it circulating around the heart until your partner feels it there too. The same with the throat and the head. Once the power hits the head you have to decide where to hold the mind, as this is where the drops will meld. Melding at the throat assists in astral projection and dream work. Melding drops at the heart cultivates awareness of interdependence: how all phenomena are composed of the five elements. Melding at the head causes spiritual ascent and wisdom. In all cases the fire must be brought all the way to the top and the upper drop melted. The final melding of drops during orgasm can happen anywhere in the body.

When orgasm does come, enter into it fully. Let go of duality, and dwell in the clear light of awareness. After orgasm, if you are both still able, you can continue to make love, or direct the energy to particular places in the body. For instance, channeling the energy to the Third Eye can lead to amazing visions and pure sight. Moving the energy to a place that needs healing can help cultivate a cure. Directing the energy toward a sigil or seal will manifest that intent.

In the male, the ejaculate will go into the bladder, but the sexual energy will be directed upward. This idea of separating the energetic essence from the physical fluid not only exists in the East, but was recognized by Western alchemists as well. Paracelsus wrote, "This emanation or separation takes place by a kind of digestion, and by means of an interior heat, which during the time of virility may be produced in man by the proximity of woman, by his thoughts of her, or by his contact with her, in the same manner a piece of wood exposed to the concentrated rays of the sun may be made to burn." Though Paracelsus was not initiated into schools of Kundalini, Tummo, Taoist Alchemy, or anything of the kind, he still saw the basic truth and process involved.

Cycling Energy

For every Tibetan Yidam you see sitting in yab yum or in union while standing, there is almost always a practice in which a mantra is generated in the heart, rises through the central channel, and is breathed into the mouth of the sang-yum,[1] where it then cycles down and through the sexual embrace back into the male. The cycle spins as you say the mantra and it generates power in line with whatever tantric deity you are working with.

During generation-stage practice this is usually done with a visualized partner, but in completion-stage practice a similar exchange of energy can take place. This spinning of energy, of one person flowing into another in an endless cycle, is a potent method for realizing gnosis and generating power that can be dedicated to practical ends. The circulation of sexual energy through the chakras of one person transmutes it into pure wisdom. The circulation through two people, around and around again, is a potent way of generating a subtle energy and substance that leads swiftly to ascension.

To perform this rite perform your invocations or establish yourself as divine as per the last chapter. Perform the Inner Fire exercise during the first part of sexual play and let the fire rise until you begin to experience the bliss descending. Continue to have sex, and begin to sync your breathing. Kiss your partner, and will the fire to enter into your partner's mouth. Your partner should cycle it down through his or her own body and back into you through the genitalia.

It doesn't matter if the woman or the man is the sender, because after a while you will switch directions. Keep switching directions every five to 10 minutes. Sex should last at least 30 to 40 minutes in order for the fire to truly sublimate all the drops and create the "steam" that fuels awakening. If you are doing this in a yab yum position (in which you are both sitting up, with the woman on the man's lap), you will start rocking back and forth in time with the cycling. This is natural and normal and should be encouraged.

Ideally, both partners should orgasm simultaneously without ejaculating, and draw the sexual fire upward. By doing this you will not only pull your refined essence upward but you will also draw sexual energy from your partner. A man will draw his woman's lunar essence and a woman will draw her man's solar essence. This combined essence, which has been heated and refined, will travel through the centers, awakening the powers of each center, creating health and stimulating spiritual growth and experience.

You can continue to cycle between you for as long as you are having your orgasm(s), and even afterward. Remain in sexual union until you are finished. If the man is using the lower lock to retain semen he may be able to resume sex immediately without even pulling out. If he is using the three-finger lock, he will have retained semen, but lost the erection.

Experiment with Cycling Through Different Centers

The energy-cycling experiment I just detailed is the simplest form of this practice. With time you will note that you and your partner are connected at many different points, and you can form a loop between any of them. For example, cycling between your hearts and navels—sending energy heart to heart and receiving it through the navel chakra directly—will create a tight emotional bond and also assist in perceiving the illusory nature of reality. Creating a loop between the genitals and Third Eye will help cultivate astral sight, projection, and lucid dreaming. Creating a wider loop between the star and earth centers that lie outside the physical body will speed one's spiritual ascent and connect one further to the heavenly powers and chthonic realms.

You can also perform cycling using oral stimulation. In fact, in my opinion, the best results come from this technique, because when you change cycling directions both partners are experiencing the same sensation: energy traveling either up or down the body. Also, you have greater control over who orgasms when, because many women can only achieve orgasm through oral stimulation and men can warn their partners when they are getting close to orgasm.

We will be revisiting this oral technique in the next chapter on working with the Elixir.

Revisiting Sex Sigil Magic

In the chapter on masturbation and magic I spoke about the now-infamous sigil magic technique in which a sigil is created to represent a sorcerous intent and is activated by the moment of orgasm. In solo sex magic this rite is powered by the energy release and "gnostic" mindset that is generated during orgasm. When doing this practice as a couple, the sigil truly becomes the magical "child" generated by this act. There are a few factors to take into account with this practice.

The first description I ever read of doing sex sigil magic as a couple suggested placing the sigil several places around the room so that whatever position you are in, it will always be near your line of sight. This is a good idea, but even at the young age of 17 I had a better one: body paints. Paint the sigil all over each of you in the appropriately colored body paint. This has a triple benefit: it actually charges your bodies as tools of the operation itself, it allows you to keep your attention on your partner (which is where you want it), and it makes for fun foreplay. I remember one operation that used day-glo body paints and an octogram marked out on the floor in day-glo orange tape. We lit the temple in black light and everything but the sigils faded into the background. It looked like some kind of psychedelic movie from the '60s but it worked its magic.

The gods you choose to invoke for this process should be in accord with the result you are attempting to achieve. For example, if you are doing a rite to find work or to find peace at home, doing a sex magic rite in which Eros has sex with Chaos is probably not going to be a good idea.

Lastly you need to choose *how* to use the energy. You can use all the techniques I've given and manifest the sigil internally at whatever centers in which you choose to meld the drops. The throat center would be good for situations in which elegant speech and influence might be useful; the heart is good for general matters and for emotional connection; the navel is good for general and material needs; the sex center is good for lust and forced enchantment.

If using the cycling method, the sigil or a sentence that you chant during the rite can be visualized as a mantra chain or symbol that moves through your channels, increasing power with the intensity of its spin. At the moment of release, if both people orgasm at the same time, you should release the sigil and just see it fly out of both of you and go manifest itself in reality. If you do not orgasm at the same time, the sigil or mantra chain should pass to the person who does orgasm, and the other person should do everything in his or her power to release the rite to that person so that the sigil can launch. If the working primarily affects one of you rather than both of you, it may be preferable to have that person release the sigil.

As to fluid retention, speaking strictly from the perspective of this operation, some claim that the release of the fluid is more beneficial because you are sending something out into the world symbolically and literally. Others have found that holding in the semen creates a more potent orgasm and allows greater channeling and patterning of the energy and a better result overall. Certainly if a man is attempting to conserve force over the long term by not ejaculating at all, it is not worth breaking that just for one spell. We will revisit this technique again in the next chapter where I talk about the use of sexual fluids in magic.

Sex Magic and Divination

In the last section I discussed how the energy in sex can be diverted to achieve particular sorceries rather than simply used for spiritual advancement. The mind-state created by the orgasm can also be used for magic, most especially divination. That moment of ego-shattering awareness, that little death, brings you right in line with eternity and clarity. That is why it is considered so powerful in tantra: enlightenment is not necessarily the fruit of lifetimes of hard work; it can be just an orgasm away. In this moment of orgasm you can, if you choose, pose a question and receive an answer in the form of a vision. Some use a sigil to represent the question, but I have found that simply repeating it to myself right at the beginning convulsions of orgasm, or, even better, having a partner pose it while falling into orgasm, works better. Often what happens is that the visions occur as your mind makes the journey from the mindshatter back to the normal waking state. These can be spoken as they are happening, or, if that would disturb your trance, be left alone and recorded from memory after the fact.

As you may have guessed, this is a practice in which the quality of the orgasm matters a lot, so mastering the techniques of prolonging sex, deepening orgasm, and meditation all come into play here.

This is one area where, if it is a man seeking the vision, semen release seems to work much better than semen retention. I have had visions both ways. When retaining and practicing Inner Fire I send the energy from the orgasm up the central channel and into the Third Eye and temples. These three points form a triangle that helps generate psychic visions. The problem is that Inner Fire and semen retention usually have their own visual effects, at first producing colors and mist, but eventually breaking down reality so much that it can be difficult to see across a room for several minutes afterward. If you release the seed during this practice, and then collapse into a laying position, the release of pressure can give way to spectacular visions if your eyes are closed or, better, if you are blindfolded. If this is your first release after a long period of chastity or retention, the effect can truly be overwhelming.

The same general rules apply to women: they can use the locks and will to send the energy of the orgasm up the central channel into the Third Eye or they can simply release and let go. Because of the greater capacity for multiple orgasms and the general intuitive nature of women, many believe women to be better suited to this technique than men. As with most claims that attempt to pigeon-hole a gender into this or that role, I find common wisdom a little too simple, and therefore suspect, but I have not done any hard studies to prove otherwise. I know of at least one couple in which the woman leads the operations and the man does the scrying and visionary work. They seem to do quite well for themselves.

If visions do not come in the moment of orgasm they may arrive during sleep. This is one time that it may be preferable to nod off to sleep right after an orgasm.

Eroto-Comatose Lucidity

Speaking of orgasmic sleep, you may have heard about some-thing called "eroto-comatose lucidity," in which a practitioner of sex magic is put into a state somewhere between sleep and wakefulness through repeated sexual stimulation. The name is so memorable, and the act even more so, that it has gained a mention in almost any book on sacred sex or sex magic in the last 30 years. The technique, under that name at least, was popularized by Aleister Crowley, though it was taught to him by his student Ida Nelidoff. As with most sex sorcery that comes through Crowley and the OTO, the American Magus Paschal Beverly Randolph did it first. He called it "The Sleep of Sialam," and Crowley and Blavatsky then correctly spelled it as Siloam: the name of the pool in Jerusalem where Jesus restored sight to a blind man. Jason Augustus Newcomb notes in his book *Sexual Sorcery* that this name is chosen to indicate that the lucidity is a restoration of your own true spiritual sight, to which you had previously been blind.

The method involves multiple sexual partners focusing on a single magician, trying to exhaust him sexually, and send him into a trance sleep. There is some question whether the ministrations of the partners should bring the primary operator to orgasm multiple times or if he or she should simply be aroused perpetually, but I am inclined to think the former because we are, after all, going for a state of complete exhaustion.

Upon the first sleep of exhaustion the group then attempts to awaken the sleeper through sexual stimulation, but stop every time he or she awakens. This continues until the primary magician falls into a deeper sleep-like trance that is characterized by transcendent awareness that is not bound by time or space. From here the magician may divine, travel astrally, or just explore the state.

I will be honest here and admit that this is one of the only things I have not done. I tried with a single partner, but she got tired, and after I entered the initial sleep, I found the awakening arousal and then stopping to be annoying rather than trance-inducing. Perhaps it might be different with a group.

Whether Ida Nelidoff knew about it or not, the ritual has similarities to Yoni-Tantra rites involving a Gopi Chakra or a group of six women worshipped sexually by a man. There is also a Pancha Chakra, or circle of five, mentioned in many tantras such as the Mahanirvana Tantra, the Nirutara Tantra, and the Yoni Tantra. In some cases the women are said to be in all different castes, whereas other tantras call for the five women to be the daughter, sister, mother, sister-in-law, and wife of the main celebrant. Obviously such an act would be illegal in most countries and considered deeply immoral by most people—myself included. Whatever the makeup of the group, the role of multiple women is not only to sexually exhaust the male and bring him into a state of maharaga, but also to serve as the various aspects of the great goddess, and provide sufficient female sexual fluids to make the Elixir described.

CHAPTER 8

The Elixir of Life:
The Sorcery of Sexual Fluids

The Sixth Dalai Lama, Tsangyang Gyatso, is famous for refusing to become a monk, having scandalous encounters with bar maids, and for writing erotic poetry. There is a wonderful story about how he avoided becoming a monk: Supposedly he was receiving a lot of pressure from the ministers and regents to stop his carousing and take monk's robes. He asked them to meet him on the roof of the Potala Palace so he could discuss the matter of his purity. Once on the roof, Kundun took a piss off the side and let it bounce from one rooftop to the next until it was just a foot from the ground—at which point he sucked it all back up into his penis! He turned to his ministers and told them that if they could control their fluids like that, then they too could maintain purity while still enjoying the company of women.

This story is meant to show that not only could the Dalai Lama control his seed, but he had in fact mastered Vajroli Mudra, a technique that allows you to draw both male and female sexual fluids into the penis. This level of working with the physical sexual fluids of semen, vaginal fluids, and menses, sometimes called "Outer Alchemy," is actually an older practice than the "Inner Alchemy" of working with the energies and mindstate of the sex act. In fact, it is one of the oldest strata of magic in general. This makes perfect sense if you place yourself in the mind of ancient man: if these fluids are the prima materia of which life is made, then their magic must be truly powerful.

We will be taking a closer look at the Vajroli Mudra that the sixth Dalai Lama demonstrated in the story later in the chapter. For now, let's examine the fluids themselves.

The White Drops

The white drops spoken of in this book, and in traditional Tantra, are the spiritual essence contained in semen. As noted in the last chapter, Paracelsus held the seminal fluid in high regard: "All the organs of the human system, and all their powers and activities, contribute alike to the formation of semen. The semen is, so to say, the essence of the human body, containing all the organs of the latter in an ideal form."[1]

In and around the Mediterranean, rain was thought to be the semen of the sky god, necessary for the fertilization of crops. Aeschylus wrote, "The pure sky yearns passionately to pierce the earth. Rain falls from the bridegroom Sky, impregnating the earth, and she brings forth her brood for mortal man."[2] In Papau New Guinea semen is used for all kinds of magic, from rubbing it into ritual scars for protection to baking it into cakes or drinking it with coconut as an aphrodisiac. So powerful is semen thought to be in that country that sometimes wives are sent to collect it from other men so that there is enough of a supply for all the varied uses. All on its own, semen is a potent force, and we will see throughout the chapter how it can be used as an anointing oil, a libation, and an offering.

Various methods for cultivating the seed in places other than a vagina have been used. For example, the OTO's 11th degree is largely dedicated to the cultivation of sperm in the anus. Contrary to popular conception that ritual need not be done by two men, and there is some evidence in Crowley's diaries that he used the anus of both men and women in 11th-degree rites. In some writings the point seems to be to cultivate the sperm alone, and in others it seems to be to combine it with blood that seeps in from tearing in the anus and remnants of feces. In this theory the blood attracts the demons and the sperm brings them to life. In 1946 Crowley wrote in his diary that he dreamed "of giving birth to a foetus per anum. It was a mass of blood and slime. The nastiest Qliphotic experience I can remember."[3]

Austin Osman Spare used what he called an "earthenware virgin" for incubating the sperm. He created a clay vessel to fit the size and specifications of his penis with just enough room left over for sperm. It had to be so tight that the suction would provide the stimulation. The sigil of the intent would be in the bottom of the virgin, and would be fertilized by the seed. The whole thing would then be buried on a quarter moon, and dug up again on the full. At that point you can refill the virgin and spill the contents on the ground to release the created spirit. Spare notes that the technique is dangerous, and always effective. I sometimes wonder if the danger he is speaking about is magical, or if the danger that comes from trying to get your penis out of something that is supposed to be so tight that it creates enough suction to stimulate you sexually.[4]

Whether drawn directly from the penis after sex or cultivated in another type of alchemical vessel, the magic potential of sperm is great. The idea of cultivating sperm alone is attractive to some homosexual men, and I believe that the alchemies and potential of this are under-explored. Sadly, so much of sacred sex and sexual alchemy between people of the same gender has had to have been kept underground or has been purposefully destroyed, and some mysteries may never be recovered.

The Red Drops

Similar to semen, female sexual fluid has a long and celebrated history in magic, witchcraft, and tantra. In Buddhist tantra the female fluids are called the "red drops," or Rakta, and are sometimes called the Red Dragon in Taoist Nudan texts that focus on women's inner alchemy. Because the menses are the only female fluid that can be seen outside the body, it was treated as sort of analogous to semen. Aristotle saw it as the basic building block of life, which is given form by sperm. In the case of sex magic, the red drops can be female sexual lubricant, ejaculate, or actual menses. It all carries the essential lunar/female energy.

The use of menses in witchcraft is quite well known. Both Italian Strega and American Hoodoo practitioners have been known to use it in spells to attract love and feed it to men in order to control them and keep them from straying. Pliny even reports that in Imperial Rome men would use it to ensure the fidelity of their wives.[5] In some cases menses are treated as a weapon both for cursing and for defense. The Kwakiutl tribe native to what is now British Columbia have been known to keep menstrual blood in bark amulets and use it as poison against monsters when traveling.

Often in the West we see a vilification of menstrual blood and menstruating women as an impure and even corrupting influence. There are innumerable taboos all over the world against women praying, entering temples, or interacting with men, during the period just before and during menstruation. At this time the woman is seen as unclean not just because she is bleeding or about to bleed, but because she cannot conceive during this time. Many wise and wary sorceresses have noticed that this is also the time that they feel an increase in libido and magical power—thus, fear of women's power surely plays a part in some of these proscriptions. Some sorceresses have commented that whereas their "time of the month" is a good time for men to gain access to a woman's creative power, or gynergy, it is actually the time just before menstruation when she holds the most power within herself.

In the tantras the menses tend to be revered rather than reviled. In Indian tantras the female fluid is treated with deep respect, and it is sometimes referred to as Kundapushpa, or "flower of the holy well" (note the *Kunda*, as in *Kundalini*). The red drop that ignites the Inner Fire is said to be the red drop we inherit from our mothers. It is synonymous with the female sexual fluid/menses. The role of female sexual fluids is even more important in Shakta Tantra, in which the female is considered the active element and the male is a corpse until animated by her.

In Aleister Crowley's system of sexual magic, menstrual blood is extremely important, and the "cakes of light" consumed as a Eucharist in his gnostic mass contain the menstrual blood of the priestess. In his *Liber Al Vel Legis* it is written that "The best blood is of the moon, monthly; then the fresh blood of a child, or dropping from the host of heaven; then of enemies; then of the priest or of the worshippers; last of some beast, no matter what." This consumption of the fluids as a Eucharist is important and will be dealt with in the next section more extensively.

Just as working alchemy with only the sperm might be a desirable mystery for gay men to explore, working with the female sexual fluids is desirable for gay women. Amazingly there is even less information on this than there is on gay male fluid magic. Even the scientific understanding of what exactly female ejaculate is, is lacking. In researching this book I was shocked to find conflicting reports claiming it to be prostatic fluid, fluid from the uterine lining, fluid from fallopian tubes, secretions of sweat into the vulva, secretions of the sebaceous glands, mucus from the cervix, or even urine. Science can, and I hope *is*, hashing this out. To the sex magician it is the Dew of Ecstasy.

The Elixir

Now that we have spoken about the fluids individually we need to discuss the Elixir, which is constructed from the combined white fluid of the man with the red flow of the woman. The Elixir of Life that grants youth and immortality has been sought by Alchemists for more than 2,000 years in both the East and the West. Most have sought to create it using minerals and plants in varying combinations, but some have seen that the chemical marriage necessary for its creation is not merely a code for a chemical process, but an actual sexual coupling. Sexual alchemists believe that the Red King and White Queen written of in the Rosary of the Philosophers may be code for the union of Sulphur and Mercury, and, at a deeper level, Sulphur and Mercury are code for the sexual fluids.

In China most of Waidan, or external alchemy, is done with minerals and plants, and the sexual powers are reserved for Neidan internal Alchemy, but in India, Nepal, Tibet, and Japan there are strong traditions of working with the sexual fluids as the Elixir. In the West many classical alchemists such as Cagliostro and Comte de Saint-Germain have been suspected of sexual alchemy, it was not until Paschal Beverly Randolph, Crowley, Naglowska, Kellner, and other sex magicians of the 19th and 20th century that this interpretation of alchemy was written about bluntly, albeit mostly within the documents of magical orders and closed circles.

Once you start working with the Elixir you see it has been hinted at everywhere. The Red and White Drops, The Rose and Cross, the marriage of the Red King and White Queen in alchemical texts, the Amrita and Rakta on the altar of Tibetan Buddhists, even the "blood and sweat" of Christ in the Holy Grail is a hint at this secret.

As to what it does, the Elixir of Life has been credited with restoring youth, granting immortality, cultivating spiritual progress, creating life from nothing, and curing all disease. I think we can safely dispute the idea of the Elixir granting physical immortality; there is a long list of Chinese emperors who died early of mercury poisoning from the very concoction that was meant to prolong their life, and Aleister Crowley's ashes are currently fertilizing a tree at a dairy farm in New Jersey[6] rather than revolutionizing society with the industrial use of semen.[7] Nonetheless, the spiritual value and magical potential of the Elixir cannot be understated. It can act as a catalyst for all manner of spiritual practices from yoga and meditation to prayer and astral travel. It can be used for anointing and empowering talismans, as well as bringing to "life" spirits and artificial elementals.

The basic process for creating the Elixir is simple enough, and the alchemical terms have been explained in the papers of secret orders that you can probably find online, and also in widely published books. From P.B. Randoph to Aleister Crowley to D.M. Kraig, Western teachings on sexual alchemy treat the heating process necessary for creating the Elixir as being simply the sex itself and thus stress making the sex act longer than the average two- to six-minute experience most couples have. Certainly a longer period of sexual union is needed, and Kraig's 40 minutes is a good mark to strive for, but it is the *inner* heat practice that is the real key to achieving this transformation from Prima Materia to Elixir. I want to say it again because this is the key to making most of the magic in this book work: ***the Inner Fire practice is the key to success.*** Yes, it is important to see yourself as empty and divine. Yes, it is important to hold the goal in mind. Yes, it is important to not let it become an empty sex session rather than a holy rite. But more important than all of this is cultivation of the Inner Fire—at first cultivated alone, and then in union with a partner.

Inner Heat and Elixir Creation

If you want to create the Elixir, you should first enter the chamber and perform your invocations either silently or aloud. As discussed earlier, this can be the invocation of a specific god or the unlocking of your own true nature, which is inherently divine and naturally clear and radiant.

You should then face each other and perform the Inner Fire exercise, letting the fire rise through heart, throat, and head. It is *only* when the fire is at the head and the descending bliss starts that you should move toward each other and embrace.

You can move through the Exploring and Flowing exercise or simply come together in union. Despite what you have read elsewhere about being free from lust or focused purely on enlightenment, the sex play *should* be passionate. Even if you cannot maintain Vase Breathing, or what Christopher Bradford poetically calls "Vulcanic Breaths," during the entire session, you should pause long enough to maintain the rising heat and descending bliss. The locks and breath-holding will be less important than maintaining this deep Vulcanic Vase Breathing. When locks are employed they should be synched to love play so that the lower locks the man is performing lift the penis pleasantly inside the woman, and the lower lock of the woman squeezes the shaft of the penis. Although it is not necessary to have *mastered* every technique, each person should have competency enough to perform without detracting from the overall sex act.

The rite should extend for a significant stretch of time; shoot for 30 to 60 minutes. Because of this length of time, your love-making technique can and should alternate during the rite. Talk to one another and let each other know what will work and what doesn't. Again we have a situation in which men will have to go to great lengths to fight off orgasm and women will sometimes have to go to great lengths to achieve it. This means that men will have to overcome the autopilot desire to just thrust hard and fast. There are a lot of factors that are under your control. For example:

☆ **Angle:** Angling your thrust upward can increase your chances of hitting her G-spot. Angling downward can sometimes let you stimulate the clitoris with your penis or even pelvis.

☆ **Speed:** Men can either start and end fast, or start slow and speed up as they move along. If you want to create the Elixir you need to learn to switch it up several times during a session: speed up, back off, and even pause to work on the locks and breath if they get lost.

☆ **Depth:** Yeah, I know the old joke: If she screams "faster" or "harder," you can oblige, but there is not much you can do when she screams "Deeper!" By depth I mean actually alternating between shallow penetration and deeper penetration. Having her squeeze the head of your penis with her vaginal muscles during shallow thrusts is yet another good way to stave off orgasm.

You might have noticed that I have not covered sex positions yet. If you flip through the book you will find no catalogue of Kama Sutra drawings or anything like that. There certainly is significant lore about different positions, but I find most of it to be bunk. Just focus on positions that aid what you are trying to accomplish. Reverse cowgirl will usually provide deepest penetration and allow upward angling. Doggy style also can have deep penetration but results in a downward angle. Yab-Yum will be excellent for slow rocking and milking.

Let your intuition, divine influence, and physical desires determine your position. Forcing yourselves into stressful poses that you can barely hold is not good lovemaking. Only you know your bodies and what you are capable of. Books that focus on exotic positions give the impression that only those at the peak of physical health can do this work, but that is not true. The Elixir can be prepared in almost any position. Those of you who want to experiment will find lots of information in some of the books listed in the bibliography.

When you both feel that it is best to orgasm, then do so. If you are creating the Elixir, then this is a case when you would not want to retain semen, though some experienced practitioners can release just a small amount of fluid and retain the rest to channel within the body. Once transmuted by the holy heat and concentration, the sexual fluids combine in the vulva and become the famed Elixir of Life.

So now you have this thing called the Elixir sitting in your or your partner's vulva. This leads us to two important questions: how do we get it out, and what does it do?

Withdrawing the Elixir with the Penis

We now come back to the story of the sixth Dalai Lama and his ability to use Vajroli Mudra to suck his urine back into his bladder. This story is obviously myth, but the practice of withdrawing fluid into the penis is real enough. In fact, medical schools in Mumbai occasionally bring in Yogis to demonstrate the technique to students.[8] I myself have seen it done in Pashupatinath, Nepal, on ShivaRatri, the night of Shiva, in 2000. A Sadhu with a small metal catheter in his penis dipped it into some kind of flammable liquid, sucked the liquid into his penis, then expelled it back out again into a candle flame, making a nice-sized fire ball. It was certainly a crowd-pleaser, but it also demonstrated a technique that has been part of sexual magic for more than 1,000 years.

The Vajroli, or Thunderbolt Technique, is an extension of the technique learned in the lower lock we use in the Inner Heat method. As with that method the stomach should be empty and the bladder should have been recently emptied. In this technique we again inhale, but this time we draw energy up the spine during the inhale and hold it at the crown or Third Eye. The abdomen is drawn back and most importantly up. At the same time you must pull up on the sexual organs using the same muscles you use in the lower lock, but this must be more forceful and with a greater emphasis on the upward motion. Women can also do this by focusing on the area just beneath the clitoris. During one inhalation, rather than simply holding this position, you pump the genitals and abdomen 10 times or so, which creates suction in the bladder, and a forceful energetic pump up the spine.

Men training in this method usually place a cloth on the top of the penis so that they know that they can build the muscles. When they build it strong enough, they wet the cloth to add more weight—the same principal as other weight lifting.

Once you master the pumping you can practice withdrawing fluid. I was taught to insert a thin rubber tube as a catheter and begin by withdrawing lukewarm milk from a bowl. Eventually you move to thicker liquids, then to the combined elixir placed into a dish, and, eventually—in theory—to the Elixir right from the vulva. The problem here is that, as James Mallinson points out in his essay "Yoga and Sex: What is the purpose of the Vajrolimudra?" to actually withdraw the Elixir physically without a tube is nearly impossible. It has never been demonstrated without the use of a tube, and, more than this, the texts never promise that it can be done without a tube.[9] Today, yogis who display the technique use a rubber catheter, but most texts, from purely yogic texts like the Dattatreyayogasastra and Hathayogapradipika to tantric texts like the Chandamaharosana Tantra, refer to a metal tube of either silver or brass. It is hard to imagine that anyone would have sexual intercourse with a metal tube in their penis for even 1 minute, much less 30 or 40 minutes.

This problem of absorbing the Elixir directly from the genitals is of course one-sided, as it is established in the vagina. For women it is a matter of simply doing Vajroli and Inner Heat to direct the sexual essence of the Elixir upward through their channels. For men this is tricky business. We either have to accept that the Vajroli technique is performed by withdrawing from the vagina, inserting a tube, and delving back in, *or* that the technique is used to separate spiritual essence from the physical substance, and is thus more or less a type of internal alchemy such as was practiced in the last chapter.

In my own experience, Vajroli is a very powerful way to absorb the essence of the Elixir, but if you want to partake of the physical substance you should use another method of retrieval instead of or directly after applying Vajroli.

Before we leave this topic I have to note that Vajroli Mudra has been connected to several sex abuse scandals involving different gurus and unsuspecting women. Many sex magicians of the late 18th and early 20th century sought to marginalize the role of the woman in sex magic, treating her more or less as a passive ingredient where the seed of sperm could take root. In some cases, such as in Crowley's *Emblems and Modes of Use*, the woman need not even be told that there is any sort of magic or alchemy afoot. This idea is not only common in the West, either; I have met two different teachers of Tibetan Buddhism who have suggested the same thing—that the woman need not be told that she is engaged in a tantric rite. While I consider this kind of shady, if all you are doing are some breath techniques for Inner Heat, meditating on the moment of orgasm, and other similar techniques, I suppose I can see how some might think it is okay not to tell their female partner. In the case of Vajroli Mudra, however, the male is removing fluid and/or energy from the female. When the male is a master at the technique and the female is either unaware or a young student with little experience, this seems unethical at best. At worst it is vampiric, and indeed Vajroli has been used as part of a strategy of cult control that we have already talked about: by absorbing the sexual essence of a person, you can funnel it to different centers in the body where it can be manipulated and used in mind-control sorcery. Such techniques are beyond the scope of what I wish to teach; suffice it to say that they exist and are devastatingly effective.

Oral Consumption

A much more feasible method of obtaining the Elixir is for the male to suck it out orally. (The rhyme of *elixir* with *he licks her* has been a source of much amusement.) In the Chandamaharosana Tantra we read the following instruction: "She should have him suck her Lotus and show his pleasure. Inhaling the fragrance, he should enter with his tongue, searching for the Red and White secretions. Then she should say to him: Eat my essence! Drink the Waters of Release! O Son, be a slave as well as a father and a lover. This is the best diet, eaten by all Buddhas."[10] Indeed, not just the Elixir, but other bodily fluids are used in tantra. The Chandamaharosana Tantra asks, "Can you bear my dear, to eat my filth and feces and urine; and suck the blood from inside my bhaga?" This, however speaks to a larger tantric practice of transcending duality, and goes beyond the topic of sexual alchemy.

This method of sucking the Elixir out with the mouth, and then sharing it either through a kiss or mixing it with wine is exactly what is prescribed in Western sex magic texts such as the OTO document "Emblems and Modes of Use." Other things sometimes get added to the Elixir, such as mercury, ashes of relics, and so on. In Crowley's gnostic mass the Elixir is baked into cakes of light along with honey and other ingredients. Kaula Tantrics make an elixir specifying five ingredients of human ash, female nectar, menses, semen, and ghee.

I strongly caution against unwise experimentation with ingredients. Even if you are in India and dealing with the most authentic guru you should not assume that Amrita or medicine pills are safe as they often have dangerous levels of mercury in them. Same with drinking from the Ganges, in fact: the blessing may be that it liberates you spiritually, but the cost for a Westerner is often a case of giardia. There are other ways.

Mutual Oral Sex

Though not written about in any tradition that I have examined, experience has shown that the Elixir can be created by two people performing mutual oral sex with each other and cycling energy in a loop as per the instructions in the last chapter.

Each person collects the heated drops in his and her mouth so that the woman holds the white drops of the man and the man holds the red drop of the woman. This situation is reminiscent of the yin-yang symbol, in which each side holds a seed of the opposite inside it.

You then come together in a kiss and share the fluids with each other, passing it back and forth, using the mouth as the place where the Elixir comes together. You may then swallow the Elixir or hold it under your tongue to be absorbed.

Anointing

The Elixir has other uses than simple consumption. It can also be used as an anointing oil on the body. The Yoni Tantra recommends drawing a line of menstrual blood and semen on the forehead. Other instructions speak of rubbing it into the chakra points to aid in loosening the knots. Applications of it for healing are likewise promised when combined with certain mantras. Unfortunately there are some texts that I am not able to quote directly because of vows, but the process is simple enough and can be adapted by the cunning sorcerer or sorceress. One modern text I *can* quote is the "Solar Wet Alchemical Way" by Christopher Bradford, the director of the Ordo Octopi Nigri Pulveri (OONP), a modern alchemical order that combines Western and Eastern methods. He writes:

> After performing the Great Rite—the true conjunction of the Sun, Moon, and Earth—the Elixir should be collected from the Chalice, the Chamber of Creation...the female alchemist's womb (which is her alchemical apparatus), within which the conjunction takes place. Take up the joined fluids, the Elixir of Life, [and] anoint the very top of the head with it. This is where the Microcosmic Mercury of the alchemist joins with the greater Mercury, the Sea of Mind. The Elixir can be diluted or dissolved into a small amount of wine, or other alcohol-based solution for penetration and ease of application.
>
> Sit in prayer after applying the Elixir, with the eyes shut, back straight, and awareness directly upon the mercurial Metal's expression at the top of the head. Be sure that it penetrates into the scalp. The nature of the Elixir is such that the Dragon will rise up into the head to meet it, and the spiritual vision will blossom. This operation is best done when the Moon is full; this being an allusion to when the female alchemist is experiencing her menses. It is effective at any time, but this time is most powerful.[11]

If one was looking for a Western magical order that taught genuine and effective techniques, one need look no further. Having had the chance to examine almost all the literature on the subject in the West, both secret and public, I can say that the OONP materials equal or surpass any of the Randolph/Crowley-derived methods, precisely because they incorporate Inner Heat and Vase Breathing, which Bradford refers to as Vulcanic Breaths.

Anointing of Talismans

The Elixir is not only for eating and anointing yourself; its properties also give "life" to talismans and other objects of the art. One merely has to perform the rite with that goal in mind and conjure the intent at the moment of orgasm so that the Elixir gives rise to that intent as the magical child.

For example, if you desire an increased ability to study, comprehend difficult intellectual material, and do well in your studies, you might make a talisman of Mercury on parchment with a stylized sigil of Mercury and perhaps a sigil of your own name as well. All rules of talisman construction for whatever tradition you follow should be obeyed up to the point of consecration. For instance, you might draw or inscribe the symbols at sunrise on a Wednesday morning, as this would be the hour and day of Mercury.

Just as you picked an auspicious time for the talisman's construction, so too should you pick an appropriate time for its consecration—perhaps the hour of Mercury that occurs during the night on the same Wednesday you constructed it.[12] For this consecration the man would invoke Hermes or Mercury into himself and his partner could invoke one of Hermes' many lovers into herself. Greek and Roman myth provides a staggeringly lengthy list that one could draw upon for this, and everyone from Hekate to Dryope (the Nymph with whom he conceived Pan) to Aphrodite (with whom he fathered Hermaphroditus) is a possibility. Though the talisman is Mercurial, the choice of partner matters and will affect how the result manifests. I would choose Hekate, as she is a mistress of magic, but Aphrodite might be an inspired choice as well, because personal influence may come into any pursuit. Another option would be for the man to invoke Mercury and the woman to simply perform the Universal Centering and rely upon her own innate divinity. Yet another option would be for no one to perform an invocation and simply dedicate the rite to Mercury at the beginning. There are options.

However you choose to do it, you would generate the Inner Heat, and engage in union, circulating energy while concentrating on the goal of the talisman. You could develop a chant for both of you to say that would represent your goal, but I would just periodically keep charging the gods to bless the rite and consecrate the talisman. If you are invoking Hermes and Hekate into yourselves then you are essentially praying to each other, or at least *through* each other to the divine power in question. I find this is best left to the heat of the moment rather than a rigid chant or invocation.

After intuition or exhaustion or uncontrolled climax occur, gather the Elixir and anoint the talisman. This is where you might want to have a prepared invocation and statement of intent. No matter what you were saying during the generation of the Elixir, this moment of consecration will solidify the purpose of the talisman and bring it to "life."

The Elixir is not only for talismans. For instance, Paschal Beverly Randolph used the sexual elixir to line the backs of scrying mirrors and sell them. The idea was that the Elixir, combined with other herbs and fluid condensers, would act as an attractor for the mirror and allow you to more easily pierce the veil into the spirit world as well as the *essential* world behind it.

One witch I know regularly anoints a hollow point at the tip of her ritual wand and a small divot inside the bottom of her ritual chalice with an elixir that she creates with her priestess. When the wand is thrust into the chalice during the symbolic great rite, there is actually some element of the *actual* great rite present to vivify the act. The same could easily be done with Wiccan traditions that use an Athame instead of a wand to represent the phallus of the god.

As we will see in the next chapter, the uses extend beyond even this, and into the rites of creating artificial beings and working with spirits.

CHAPTER 9

It's Alive!
Homunculi and Artificial Spirits

Apart from longevity, health, and spiritual advancement, sexual alchemy has been concerned with another goal: the creation of life. Because the powers of ordinary sex are what give rise to ordinary life forms, it has been reasoned that the Elixir of Life could give rise to new life with very specific magical properties. In this chapter we will be dealing with two examples of this: The creation of artificial spirits and alchemical Homunculi.

Fraternitas Saturni

Artificial Spirits are very well known in occultism and go by many names: Egregores, Servitors, Thoughtforms, Budwills, Artificial Elementals, Logismoi, and Thralls are just a few of them. They have become a staple in Chaos Magic, but are also used in other traditions. The German Magical Order Fraternitas Saturni

(FS) used the sexual elixir to give life to their artificial spirits, which they called Psychogones.

Their methods were fairly straightforward and were the work of the 18th Pentalphic Degree of that order. Two rites are described in Stephen Flowers's book *Fire and Ice*. The first one is a decidedly Saturnian spin on the classic tantric Five-M rite, which they most likely read about in Arthur Avalon's translation of the Mahanirvana Tantra. In this rite, mansa (meat), matsya (fish), mudra (grain), madya (wine), and maithuna (sex) are all partaken of as a way to free the mind and ego by violating taboos. Unless you live in a culture where all these things are taboo there is little value in including them in a rite unless you just happen to have a hankering for surf and turf and a little wine. If you do include a feast in your rite, make sure it is light, as the stomach should not be full if you are planning on generating Inner Heat as part of your work. The Fraternitas Saturni text does not specifically call for it (or anything similar to it) but it would add much to the rite.

In this rite from the FS, you would have prepared a parchment with sigils to represent the Psychogone and what you want it to accomplish. According to Flowers the temple would be decked out in black satin and upside-down pentagrams. The man sits on a low stool and the woman crouches between his legs. The Parchment is on the floor between them and gets charged with mesmeric passes and breath work. The woman, called the medium in this ritual, mounts the man and engages in sexual union. The man ejaculates into the woman first rather than a simultaneous orgasm. The woman then proceeds to have an orgasm, but the text does not describe exactly how or if it matters. She then stands over the parchment and lets the combined essence spill upon the parchment, which will form the basis of the Psychogone.

In the second rite, called Astral Procreation, the woman is lying next to the man. The woman is placed into trance using hypnotic techniques and an incense made from hashish.[1] The parchment is placed in its own circle in front of the man. Using his left hand the man begins to stroke the chakra points of the woman. His right hand is placed over the parchment and he draws power from the female medium, which gets patterned and mediated by the male magus. He then channels this into the parchment with his right hand, visualizing the shape that the Psychogone is going to take. The magician repeats massaging the medium's chakras in a sequence anywhere from seven to nine times. When this stage is complete the woman awakens from her trance, unites with the man, and again creates the Elixir. The rite concludes with the Elixir being mixed with wine and soaking the entire parchment, which is then dried off over a brazier by being smoked in an appropriate incense.

Psychogones

You can adopt the methods I just described easily enough, but there are other variations you can use. For instance, in the Astral Procreation rite, I see no compelling reason that the woman must be in trance and the man the operator. Whereas some traditions follow Aristotle's lead and consider the man to be the active principal and the woman to be nothing more than a passive ingredient for the man to pattern; others do not. In Shakti Tantra it is Shiva (male principal) that is shava (corpse-inert) without Sahkti (female active principal). To my mind it makes much more sense, in that it is closer to the process by which a child is created, for the woman to be the operator and the man to be the one that contributes energy and seed.

I know a lesbian couple who do a similar version of this rite with remarkably potent effects. They are private in their practice so I won't out them here, but when I asked about how the spirit gets "fertilized" they pointed me to research showing that eggs can be fertilized with stem cells taken from either the male of the female. The magical process is not much different, it being the will that seeds the menstruum rather than the male seed.

The same rite could be attempted by two men, and indeed we have already mentioned Crowley's ideas about the blood caused by anal tearing being a substitute for the female portion of the Elixir. As I have said before, the field of homosexual sex magic is woefully underexplored and most of what has been done has been eradicated from the record by force. If people reading this book find themselves wishing that I could go deeper on the subject, so do I. I hope that the little bit I do write can be the catalyst for more people to research, experiment, and report results.

Reasons for Creating Artificial Spirits

My own methods for creating artificial spirits would take us too far from the subject matter of this book. They are covered in my Strategic Sorcery course and in a forthcoming chapbook called "The Secret of the Tulpa." There is enough here for you to set up your own ritual process already. What I do want to talk about are general guidelines for handling artificial spirits, what you need to consider when you create them, and why you would even want to do so.

So much of the literature of magic is devoted to conjuring spirits to perform tasks that you can probably find a spirit that would be appropriate for doing just about anything you could possibly think of. With hundreds of names and seals of actual spirits at our disposal, a perfectly valid question to ask is, *Why would anyone want to create an artificial one?* In general, working with real spirits is a higher and more potent practice, so some dismiss even the need for Psychogones, but there are a few reasons for creating them:

1. **Control.** Ever wonder why some attractive and wealthy men and women hire escorts and prostitutes? It boils down to controlling a situation. They want what they want, when they want it, and they want it with no fuss and no muss. When dealing with spirits, you are dealing with other beings who have proclivities, interpretations, and taboos. But by making an artificial spirit, you have much more control over the thing (though not total) and can set as many parameters as you like for its behavior, and even its destruction.

2. **Nuance.** There are a lot of ancient spirits that one might call upon, but not many of them are devoted specifically to computer security, finding partners who are into a particular kink, providing automotive care, spreading Internet memes, or many other things that one may

find handy in the 21st century. Yes, you can usually find a spirit that you can interpret in a modern way, but you can't really say that they are designed specifically for it.

3. **To perform menial tasks.** You might not summon a demon to help you find parking spots in the city or to find a suitable apartment, but I have created servitors for both of those reasons.

4. **The creative impulse.** Different people's gifts manifest in different ways. Some people's gifts are fed by the creative act. They may have some capacity to summon and constrain spirits, but the act of creating something is really what they excel at. I myself often find that creating a spirit or a new seal or a new ritual in certain situations can be better than even the most tried and true traditional methods. This is not always the case, but it differs for different people.

5. **Just because it can be done.** Sometimes that's all there is to it. There are a dozen ways to do just about anything, and sometimes you feel more connection to one practice than another, or maybe just want to experiment. Humans owe a lot of our progress to needing no reason to explore other than "because it's there" or "because we can." Besides, it might be fun. People forget that magic can be fun—sex magic especially so!

Basic Considerations

Making artificial spirits can be as simple or as complex as you like. What you need first, though, is a reason for its existence. After you have that you can sigilize the desire as you did with the talisman. Of course, this is a little more complicated than a simple talisman, so it usually involves more than one sigil. The privately circulated papers that have emerged from the FS material show that they also relied upon parchments that had drawings of the Psychogone and several sigils.

The first step is to create the main sigil that encapsulates the purpose of the spirit. This is its heart and brain, and it should be given center spot in any parchment or vessel that is meant to anchor or house the spirit.

Once you have the main sigil, you should come up with other sigils for any rules, parameters, or special instructions. For instance, when I and Matt Brownlee, who did most of the illustrations in this book, were looking for an apartment on a very tight schedule, we created a sigil to help us find an apartment in one day. The main sigil was for this purpose. Other sigils concerned the rooms we needed, the neighborhoods we wanted to live in, the rent we could afford, and so on. This spirit worked so amazingly well we adjusted his programming for long-term pursuits and still use him for various tasks 18 years later! Matt claims that he can sense this Artificial Spirit easier and more viscerally than he can most other spirits.

I treat the main sigil as the center, and then all other sigils as limbs, which can then branch out into further limbs. In a sense you are writing the DNA or code for a spirit.

The next consideration is shape. If you are not making one to match a material host such as a statue or painting it can take any size and shape you can imagine. The shape should have something to do with its purpose, of course. A floating mass of eyeballs is great for intelligence-gathering, but not so much for defending from attack. Microscopic servitors for healing inside the body, parasitic servitors for attaching to targets, technological servitors for interacting with computers—these are all options.

The charging itself is something that can happen in numerous ways, but because this is a book on sex magic I would strongly recommend the Elixir or some combination of fluids. Using a method similar to the FS rituals or writing your own ceremony will do nicely.

Expiration Date

The common wisdom on Artificial Spirits is that they must be given an expiration date or they will run amok, turn against you, and ruin your life. Much of this comes from a story about Buddhist Alexandra David-Néel, who created what she mistakenly called a Tulpa (a thoughtform) during her travels in Tibet in the early 1900s. Her Artificial Spirit escaped her control and began to manifest to others in her party, who were unaware of her mental efforts to create one. She then had a very difficult time reabsorbing the spirit, which had changed from the friendly little monk figure she had created to a thin, sinister-looking spirit. This type of scenario can happen, but it is not likely. It is certainly not the de facto outcome of having a long-term Servitor. David-Néel's spirit had no firm purpose; it was made to see if it could be made. If you have encoded your intent into the servitor as I suggest, you will probably have no problems like this, even if you let your servitor roam free for years.

The trick is that you have to feed it. If you created it using the Elixir you should feed it the Elixir at least once a year, and preferably once a month if you plan on using it frequently. If, however, you are creating it for a single purpose, such as getting a job, increasing customer count over a quarter, or something similar to that, it is usually a good idea to give your servitors a date to dissipate. It is best if this is connected with a specific event such as an astronomical occurrence or worldly event rather than a calendar date. If you don't give it a date to dissipate, but do not continue to feed it, it may begin to take sustenance elsewhere and change its nature. There are ways to get it to fend for itself in healthy ways that support its basic programming, but those are a little more complicated and beyond the scope of this book. Suffice it to say that if it was created from sex, it will need sex to survive, and you don't want something hanging around getting vampiric every time you have sex—unless you are into that. Like I said at the beginning of the book: no judgment.

Homunculi

I would rather not have to talk about the creation of Homunculi—believe me, I would *really* like to not have to talk about it, because it's not something I want to hear of anyone who reads this book doing—but I think any discussion of sexual alchemy would be incomplete without at least mentioning it.

Homunculus literally means "Little man," and it refers to the alchemical creation of...well, a little man. This has been a goal of Western alchemy for hundreds of years. The term *Homunculus* was first used by Paracelcus in his *De Natura Rerum* (*Of the Generation of Natural Things*) in 1537. The idea kept appearing after that, from *The Chymical Wedding of Christian Rosenkreutz* to the writings Crowley made on the subject for the Ordo Templi Orientis. It is likely that Paracelcus got the general strategy from Persian Alchemist Jābir ibn Hayyān, who called it a Tawkin.

The idea is that the alchemist is learning to wield the untapped forces of nature, and emulating God's powers of creation. Through this emulation, and learning the process, the alchemist is transformed and purified. Through the act of creating the Homunculus, the alchemist ascends. Plus, you now have a little man running around, which I am sure is useful for all kinds of things.

Some Homunculi were credited with supernatural powers, which could be yet another reason for their creation. Ten Homunculi that could foresee the future were supposedly kept in the Masonic lodge in Vienna in the 1700s.

In order to create a Homunculus, Paracelsus instructs us to place sperm inside a horse's womb for 40 days until it starts to move on its own. Then you feed it human blood for another 40 weeks in the even heat of the horse's womb. Eventually you wind up with a living humanoid, only much smaller.

Crowley mentions two methods in his paper "On the Homunculus: A Secret Instruction of the 9th degree." The first is more or less the same as Paracelcus's ectopic method. The second method, which is the real focus of the paper, is why we are talking about this in a book on sex magic. In this method the Homunculus is a child that is created the normal way, and brought to term in the woman throughout the course of nine months just like a normal baby. What makes it a Homunculus is that the child is not inhabited by a human spirit but by an elemental or other spiritual power.

The process starts with the selection of the proper woman. This is an issue that comes up in tantric texts as well, but I have ignored it thus far because in the West our sex partners are going to be our lovers, and a lot of the traditional thought about "appropriate partners" is misogynistic to say the least. In this case, though, the mother has to be suited to the nature of the spirit that is to manifest. Crowley recommends that she be chosen based on her horoscope and her willingness to aid in this ill-conceived nonsense—er, I mean, alchemy. Another approach is to ritually summon a woman who is appropriate and willing to bring the child into existence. The most famous example of this is the Babalon Working, conducted by rocket scientist Jack Parsons[2] and L. Ron Hubbard[3] for the purpose of summoning the Thelemic goddess Babalon. At the climax of many days of rituals in the desert, a woman named Marjorie Cameron, an artist perfectly fitting the description of the woman Parsons was looking for, appeared at his manor (known as The Parsonage) looking for a room. She became his magical partner and lover until his death in 1952 when he was killed in an explosion.

Once the woman is chosen you would have sex repeatedly until she becomes pregnant. Once she's pregnant you whisk her away to a place where she will be surrounded by the symbolism, scents, and general atmosphere of the type of being you want to manifest in the child. You repeatedly perform banishings to keep human spirits from taking up residency in the fetus and perform invocations to draw the type of spirit you wish to manifest. The end result should be a nonhuman soul in a human form. It is believed that such beings could bring about major changes to all of mankind.

As you might have noticed by my tone, this is not a work that I would recommend. I find it objectionable in terms of both its idea and its execution. Crowley himself was not supportive of Parsons' attempts to birth a Homunculus, or "Moonchild," as he called it. I mention it only for the sake of completeness.

Are They Really Artificial?

Because the Homunculus made in this way is infused with a power summoned by the sorcerer rather than made from his or her own will and substance, you could argue that the being is not an alchemical product at all, at least not any more than any other child. It is an incarnation directed by the sorcerer rather than directed by natural processes.

Despite protests to the contrary, the Psychogone of the Fraternitas Saturni, as well as any other artificial spirits, might very well be partaking of the same process: A form is visualized in astral space, a link on the material plane is made to empower it and work with it, it is fed with the Elixir of Life, and this creates a vortex that attracts spirits or unformed intelligences similar to the way the natural sex act does. It may well be the case that a very real spirit or intelligence takes up the form and programming that you set for it. This certainly would explain some of the behaviors that artificial elementals display.

Whether this is the case or not should not matter overmuch. Just as your own essence, which exists beyond being whoever you are in this life, is deeply constrained by your physical brain and body, your diet, your upbringing, and pretty well everything that ever happens to you, so too is any intelligence that takes up residence in a Homunculus or a Psychogone. Upon death or destruction, the spirit is released to incarnate again, just like the spirit of an ordinary person who dies.

Sex with a Skull

The last rite I want to talk about that involves the creation of a new entity comes to us through the Tachikawa sect of Japan, and is easily one of the most interesting and complex uses of sexual fluids. The Tachikawa were founded in 1114 as an attempt to create a tantric sect within Shingon that practiced sex yogas like Tibetan and Indian tantric schools. Named for the town in which it was founded, this sect was outlawed in the 13th century, but survived underground until the 17th century, and some say it is still in operation today but remains very secret. Most texts have either been destroyed or are kept sealed and marked with warnings never to be opened. One person I know who claims to have seen some Tachikawa Texts in a Shingon Temple claims that they are literally bound in chains.

Though the Tachikawa sect came to many of the same conclusions as Buddhist tantrics in India and Tibet, it developed independently of the Mahasiddha tradition, and thus has unique characteristics. For instance, the Tachikawa would begin sex-relations at midnight and continue absorbed in bliss until dawn. At the moment of the sun's rise, they would both orgasm and experience the great bliss and loss of ego that comes with the Lion's Roar, their term for the orgasm.

One of the most infamous rituals they practiced is the empowerment of a human skull as a Honzon, a holy relic with supernatural powers. Skulls are nothing new in tantra, and Kapalas, bowls made from human skull caps, are quite common, and even available online for serious practitioners. The Tachikawa practice is quite different from the Indian and Tibetan Kapalika-derived traditions, however. It demonstrates the power of the Elixir to open up communication between worlds.

First the practitioner chooses a particular type of skull, such as the skull of a Shogun or an elder. (Some instructions tell you to make a skull called the Thousand Cranium Skull by making one out of bone paste made from the tops of 1,000 men's skulls.) After this the operator adds a jawbone, tongue, and teeth, and lacquers the whole thing so that it appears to have skin. He then has sex with the skull as well as with a woman. They then wipe the combined sexual fluids on the skull, and repeat this process until there are 120 layers of sexual fluids coating the whole skull.

When the skull is not being used for sex, a Frankincense-based incense called Hangonko that is reputed to summon the dead is burned within the skull, and the smoke is allowed to pour from the eyes while chants inviting the spirit of the person whose skull it was to return. After this, various talismans and herbs are placed in the skull, the outside is covered in silver and gold leaf, and multiple mandala images are painted on the skull in the combined sexual elixir. Cinnabar, long connected with Inner Heat and Chi, is rubbed into the tongue and lips.[4] Gems are placed in the eye sockets. The skull is kept in a bag stained with the menstrual blood of a virgin.

There are many versions of this ritual, some taking up to eight years to complete, and others only require a small section of skull that you can then wear as a talisman. In all cases there is a great emphasis on the sexual fluids as well as keeping the skull warm with warmth from the body.

The idea behind the ritual is that the skull contains 10 spiritual essences or souls that exist within every person. Three souls called Hun move on and reincarnate, but seven of them, lesser souls called Pó in Japanese, remain and act as dormant guardian spirits. The sexual fluids used in the ritual are thought to revive the seven remaining spirits from dormancy. The three Hun souls that were originally inhabiting the skull in life are replaced by the Hun contained in the Elixir. The combination of the old seven and three new souls, under the warming efforts of the operator and the blessings invoked by the Buddhas and Dakinis, give rise to a new being, which will grant requests for sorcerous actions.

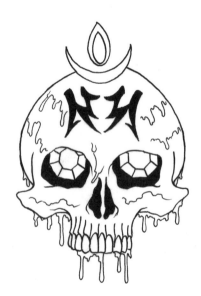

As you can see from the range of practices in this chapter, the work of animating or creating a spirit through sexual alchemy can range from very simple rites with minimal equipment, to extremely time-intensive and materially demanding processes. There are no shortcuts here, and the result is directly related to the effort that you put into it. Whether you are looking to create a servitor that will fulfill a single task then dissipate into the ether, or an artifact that will still be active long after you die is up to you.

CHAPTER 10

Raise Your Spirits:
Sex for and with Angels, Demons, Gods, and Spirits

Because the sex act attracts spirits to its vortex, gives them flesh, and eventually bears them into manifestation, it is no wonder that there are several categories of sex magic devoted to spirit communication, conjuration, and communication. In this chapter we will look at the ways sex between humans can aid communication with spirits, and then look at the many examples of humans having sex with nonphysical beings.

The Elixir as Offering

The easiest way to start this conversation is to discuss sexual fluids as an offering to spirits. Simply put, one of the oldest strata of magical practice is the making of offerings to spirits. There is no other single practice from which my students report more positive change than the making of daily offerings. I have them make offerings to four categories of recipients, or guests:

1. Gods and Ascended Beings
2. Protectors, ancestors, and important spirits of their traditions and location
3. All beings of land, sky, and underworld
4. Beings to whom we owe specific debts or whom we have offended somehow

The first and highest classification of guests served at an offering is Deity in its highest, most cosmic sense, as well as those beings that can be considered enlightened, such as Buddhas, ascended masters, Ipsissimi, and so on. This type of guest doesn't in any way *need* the offerings we make; the benefit is strictly ours. By making offerings to such beings we remind ourselves of what we constantly strive toward, and in turn build a connection to beings that have achieved that level of realization. It is an exchange similar to that between a parent and child: your child may give you something that you neither want nor need, but you accept it, and go out of your way to enjoy it fully because you know that it cultivates certain qualities in the child. This type of offering cannot be underrated.

The second classification of guest are the protectors, guardians, and lesser deities of a tradition. These are beings of great power but who are not fully realized beings. They do actually enjoy the substance of the offering that is made but do not depend upon them. This category also includes your own ancestors.

The third classification is simply all regular beings. This can include all nonphysical entities such as nature spirits, ghosts, and so on, as well as the spirits of all currently incarnated beings. It most especially appeals to beings of the land, underworld, sky, and sea of the place where you live, but in the grandest sense it is every single sentient being.

The fourth classification singles out beings to whom you owe some kind of debt. These could be problems that come from this life, with people, or with spirits. The most common example is a spirit of nature that you have run afoul of through your ordinary human actions, such as driving or getting rid of trash. A good portion of the shaman's work is keeping the balance between our world and the world of the spirits—a role that the sorcerer will sometimes be asked to fulfill. Being a magician you are even more able to trample upon the turf of spirits or powers that you may not even be aware of—one of the dangers of the endless banishing sometimes recommended by books on ceremonial magic.

In my book *The Sorcerer's Secrets*, as well as in my Strategic Sorcery course, I discuss offerings at great length, and will one day put out a book on that subject alone. Suffice it to say that most of the time offerings in ritual consist of incense, light, food, valuable items, or energy sent directly. Because sexual fluids are so powerful, personal, and are in fact a base for spirits' manifestation into the physical, some people use them as an offering to the spirits. This is a powerful practice when working with some spirits, but not a good idea in all or even most cases. There are two primary problems that you have to take into consideration.

The first problem is that in many cultures and religions, sperm, menses, and any sexual fluids are considered unclean. For instance, you might think it's a good idea to offer semen to Dionysus, Aphrodite, or Luna because of their connections to sex and fertility, but in Greek religion semen was called Miasma, and was a pollution that would cause the gods not only to not accept offerings, but to actually reject them, and, by proxy, *you*, outright. Menstrual blood has the same reputation of uncleanliness in most religions, both Pagan and Christian.[1] Invoking the deities to have sex through you and produce the Elixir is very different from asking them to accept a cup of love juice like it is vintage wine.

Some books teach that the energy released from sexual fluids is universally loved, but I have not found it to be so. More than a few people that have come to Vodou, Santeria, and other African Traditional Religions through the lens of Chaos Magic and Thelema have made these offerings only to offend the Lwa, Orisha, and spirits, and invoke their wrath. Just because you have come to a mystical understanding of the fluids, or have taken a tantric view that moves you beyond thinking of things as pure and impure, that does not mean that the beings you are working with feel the same way. At the same time there are many beings who do enjoy those substances as offerings, and I have gotten excellent response from Typhonian entities, as well as Buddhist tantric beings, for whom this type of offering is as common as the Amrita and Rakta, or white nectar and blood. There is no hard and fast rule, so just be smart. Do your research, do divinations, and tread lightly.

The second problem is that these substances are highly personal to you, and can be used to take advantage of you. There are vampiric and aggressive entities, and giving them your semen or sexual fluids is like opening a wide gateway into your deepest parts for them to influence. When you consider that one of the classes of being that you want to appease with your offering is spirits who are angry with you or to whom you owe a debt, I am sure how you can see that this might be an unwise practice. In general, dedicating a sexual act to the honor of a god or goddess is a lot safer than laying out your fluids on a platter with some cheese and a nice chianti.

If you do offer sexual fluids to a spirit, make sure that they are collected ritually, and heated up through your sexual alchemy so that they are transformed into true Elixir of Life. Lastly, if it is something that you find gross, don't offer it. You probably would not want something that was offered to you with a turned-up nose, and neither do they.

Sex for Evocation of Spirits

Apart from simple offerings, sex has been used in acts of summoning and evoking spirits as well. In most cases a spirit and seal contained within a traditional grimoire is chosen, such as one of the 72 spirits of the Goetia, or a demon from the Grimoire Verum. The ritual itself is hacked to incorporate sexual elements for both the operator and for the seer, even if they are the same person. Though I am sure it would give traditional Grimoire purists apoplexy, people have done it, and report excellent results. The degree to which a traditional ritual can be followed to the letter or changed to fit the needs of the present is a matter of ongoing debate. I myself think that operations should first be attempted in as close to a traditional manner as possible so that at least you understand what it is you are changing before you change it. After that, though, I have no great interest in sticking to a text just for the sake of sticking to it.

For the operator, the sex act is one that generates a lot of force and power; dedicating that act to any goal is potent, and the act of evocation is no different. For the seer, the ego-shattering moment of orgasm provides a unique window into trance and vision.

I am not going to give precise instructions for exactly how to do this for two reasons: First, the number of grimoires and the instructions in them are too numerous to have every nuance described; second, unless you are competent in spirit evocation *without* sex, you have no business performing it as a sexual rite. That said, an example that can be adopted to fit individual needs might look like this:

1. First is purification—both the breath purification and any baths or prayer time recommended by the grimoire.

2. Both operators should wear the sigil of the spirit, as you would during a normal evocation. Robes and other clothes can be dispensed with or replaced with bands or ribbons that are the appropriate color and nature to the work. This could be anything from a satin bathrobe to a leather catsuit. It depends upon you and the spirit.

3. Before the rite, at least one full conjuration and, even more importantly, the dismissal should be memorized. Given the strange things that sometimes happen during evocations, this is something I strongly recommend anyway. I once had papers blow off my altar and beyond the range of my circle. I distinctly heard the spirit say, *"Now what do you do, hotshot?"* Thankfully the spirit was testing me rather than attacking me.

4. You would gather together in the temple and establish preliminaries however you normally would. Whether working straight from the text, using a Golden Dawn derived system of Pentagram/Hexagram rites, or a simple circle casting, you would establish things more or less normally.

5. Engage in sexual *union* while reciting the conjuration. This should take a while, and you may even wish for sex play to start before the reading. If you incorporate methods of Inner Heat, all the better. Keep the conjuration rolling in time with the thrusting and sex play. If you lose one or the other, slow it down and get back in line. Sex should feed the power of the conjuration, not distract from it. Conjuration should channel the potency of the sex, not derail it.

6. Ideally, both participants should reach climax at the same time, but if this is not possible then the stamina of both people needs to be taken into account. If the operator is capable of multiple orgasms, then by all means he or she can orgasm first, but as we will see, the seer's orgasm is paramount. If the operator can orgasm before the seer and continue to maintain sex, then great. If not then the seer can have an orgasm afterward or not at all.

7. The orgasm of the seer is the gateway to communication with the spirit. All the same factors that come into play using the orgasm as a gateway for scrying come into play here. Often the spirit speaks when the seer is on his or her way back from the height of orgasm—that moment out of time when the ego shatters, duality collapses, and reality is beheld exactly as it is. Before returning to normal consciousness the spirit takes hold and direct communication is possible. Though others have used scrying mirrors, crystals, and triangles along with sex, in my opinion it works best as a purely psychic experience. Again, the quality and duration of the orgasm matters, so a mastery of all the techniques mentioned thus far can come into play as needed.

8. Dismissal and closing should proceed as normal. Special attention should be given to the seer to make sure that he or she is free from the spirit as much as is ever possible.

This is another operation where having one experienced person as operator and another inexperienced person as seer is inappropriate. The contact is too intimate for someone who really does not know what he or she is doing. Any operator who is experienced in this art should make sure that whomever else he or she involves is not only consenting to the sex but also to the spirit contact, and that he or she has all the facts necessary to make that decision for him- or herself.

Spectrophilia

Spectrophilia is the term used to cover attraction to ghosts, demons, and other noncorporeal or supernatural beings as well as the actual sexual relations between them. There are a lot of examples of this in almost all cultures: the Popobawa that stalks the jungles of Zanzibar raping both men and women, the Trauco of Chile who is said to be able to impregnate women with its gaze, the Incubus and Succubus of Christian demonology, and even the archangels themselves.

Many instances of night visitations are clearly ancient explanations for what we now know to be sleep paralysis, sleep apnea, or nocturnal emission. The Alp of German legend is pretty clearly an example of this: an elf that turns into mist and enters the body of the person and creates horrible dreams and experiences. Stories of Succubi or female sex demons were a convenient excuse in the Puritan world for men who got caught with wet sheets in the morning. In other cases these stories are very likely coverups or explanations for people who have been sexually assaulted. Girls with an unwanted pregnancy could claim that an Incubus or male sex demon impregnated her with semen it was given by a Succubus, who would of course have stolen it from some good Christian man. In Malaysia in the 1960s there was an outbreak of women reportedly raped by a spirit named Orang Minyak, which means Oily Man. Most people believe that he was a normal man, or a group of men that covered themselves in oil for camouflage. Reports of men covered in oil, wielding knives, and raping young virgins have continued to be reported all the way through 2012.

This being a book on sex magic, we are not concerned with explanations of wet dreams or physical stalkers. We should not even be overly concerned with examples of genuine spiritual congress that happen to people unwittingly or unwillingly. This is a book on sex sorcery and spiritual practice, so the question is: are there ways of initiating sexual contact with spectral beings, and is there any reason for doing so? Yes to both.

Demons of Top and Bottom

Let's start at the bottom and work our way up. We have already mentioned the Succubi (lays underneath) and Incubi (lays on top) as predatory demons who afflict good Christians with unwanted attention, often reportedly bringing sickness and death with them. Apart from these poor souls there have been those who have sought the company of Incubi and Succubi for their own gain.

In accounts of confessed witches during the Inquisition, several describe copulating with a demon or the Devil himself during the Sabbat. In most cases this is likely to be false testimony given under torture. Even in cases when it was a true description it might very well have been a priest in a mask of the Horned God. In other cases, however, perhaps it was a genuine description of a sexual encounter with a spiritual being, with powers granted during the exchange. Certainly the Roman Church believed that was the case, which is perhaps why, according to De Nugis Curiallium (Trifles of Courtiers), Pope Sylvester II got himself involved with a Succubus named Meridiana who was supposedly instrumental in his rise to power.

I have met some Left Hand Path Sexual Alchemists who claim to create a four-part Elixir with the fluids of both genders of humans and demons present. This Elixir, they claim, is the true work of alchemy as it not only binds together the powers of male and female, but also brings together the human and spirit worlds. If that is your thing, then it is worth considering (though it's not exactly my cup of tea).

As for the how-to of manifesting a demon lover, there are a couple of primary methods. The first is to could conjure a demon that grants familiar spirits as per the instructions of just about any grimoire. The demon will hopefully then show up and grant powers in exchange for, or through the agency of, sexual intercourse. Another method would be to seek out such lovers in a trance state, during astral travel, or in the dream state. This would not be in ordinary dreams but lucid dreaming to perform works of magical training, practical sorcery, and conscious exploration. This method of dream control to seek spirit lovers is taught by Kenneth Grant in his book *Cults of the Shadow*, where he calls it "Sexo-Somniferous Magnetization." I am pretty sure he was trying to one-up Crowley's "Eroto-Comatose Lucidity" with that one.

There are numerous techniques for achieving the lucid dream state, and it doesn't matter whether you follow a method from modern psychology, Tibetan Dream Yoga, or an article from the 'net, so long as you are able to wake up within the dream to the fact that you are in a dream, and do it without physically waking up. Meditation helps a lot, as does the practice of constantly asking whether or not you are dreaming, so that the question becomes so habitual that you will ask yourself in a dream, and the answer will of course be yes.

The method I have had the most success with is pledging that I will become lucid right before bed, and remembering it during the dream state. This is what psychologists call the MILD method, or Mnemonic Induction of Lucid Dreams.[2] When I am very serious about the work I set my alarm to ring about five hours into a night of sleep. After I go to the bathroom I get back to bed and focus all intent on lucidity. Because the REM cycle is longer later in the night, you take advantage of the prime time to become lucid. This aids in achieving lucidity as well as holding it. Studies in lucid dreaming have shown a 60-percent increase in success using this technique. Upon achieving lucidity in the dream I rub my hands together and spin around. Stephen La Burge, a noted psychologist who focuses on lucid dreams, has noted that 90 percent of lucid dreams can be lengthened by having dreamers rub their hands together. Spinning was shown to have a 96-percent effectiveness rate.

Once in the lucid state you call out to the astral to find your demonic lover. You follow signs, you pray to Demon Rulers, whatever it takes. There are no hard and fast rules. What should be clear is that the relationship and physical effects of it should not merely be a dream. When this actually occurs there is a physical manifestation that accompanies any trance or dreamlike state. In other words, the sex is real, not a dream.

Lucid dreaming has many other uses in magic, and even in the case of seeking a partner for lucid dreaming, your tastes may not run to the demonic. You may be looking for something a little more nature-based.

Learning to Love Your Elf

Similar to the demonic Incubus and Succubus, spirits of nature are also known to have sexual relations with people, and, also similar to demons, these arrangements can be unwanted, essentially amounting to rape.

In the case of women, Faeries would not just have sex with them, but would abduct them. Some believe it was just from desire; others claim that the Fairy Folk need red blood to enter heaven. From the Irish tale of Ethna the Bride we learn that "The fairies, as we know, are greatly attracted by the beauty of mortal women, and Finvarra the king employs his numerous sprites to find out and carry off when possible the prettiest girls and brides in the country. These are spirited away by enchantment to his fairy palace at Knockma in Tuam, where they remain under a fairy spell, forgetting all about the earthly life..."[3]

Often the fairies would leave changelings, or fairy offspring, in the place of the humans they stole. The changelings would then get sick and die, thus throwing off the trail of the mortal husband and family. The most famous example of this was in 1895 when Bridget Cleary was murdered by her husband, father, aunt, and cousins. She had become ill and her family assumed that she had been abducted and a changeling left in her place. They killed her during torture sessions aimed at getting the changeling to reveal where the real Bridget was.

Female faeries would also visit men, though rarely abduct them. One such faerie, the Leanhaun Shee, was said to trap her lovers until they found a replacement. If, however, you refused her advances, she would become your faerie slave.

Similar to demons, though, not all Faerie and elf sex was unsolicited. In Iceland a full 60 percent of the population believes in the Huldufolk (Hidden Folk), or elves: roads have been diverted to avoid elf grounds, shamans are hired by businesses to help avoid upsetting elves with new buildings and environmental impact, and there is even an elf school to teach people about the lore and practices of the Hidden Folk. Locals believe that elves manifest both as spirits and as physical beings—is it any wonder then that folks would turn to the elves for sex?

Hallgerður Hallgrímsdóttir, a self-described "elf nerd," has been writing about her sexual experiences with the elves. In her book, *Please YoursELF: Sex with the Icelandic Invisibles*, she reports that they have the capacity to read your mind and always know what you need in the way of sexual love. She also reports that because of their light and flexible bodies they are capable of sexual positions impossible for humans.[4] As to the *how* to of attracting an elf or fairy lover, Hallgrímsdóttir recommends finding a mossy grove on midsummer's eve, stripping naked, and rolling around in the moss and grass. If you wish it, and the Hidden Folk are into it, they will show up and make love to you.

If you are not so fortunate to live in a place where there are physical elves and fairies around, I would recommend meeting one in the same way that you might meet a human lover: by holding a nice dinner party. Of course, this would be a feast for the spirits, not for your neighbors. Lay out some incense, candles, fruit, bread, and other items you think might be enjoyed by the spirits of nature. Avoid meat or even incense that has musk or animal product in it, as some classes of nature spirits are fiercely vegetarian. There are a lot of rituals, both new and old, for making offerings of this type. In Tibetan Buddhism, bhumipati offerings to the spirits of a place are a daily occurrence. Even Ceremonialist Agrippa recommends relating to the elementals and nature spirits through offerings. In other books I describe offerings in great detail, but all you really need to do is find a nice spot outdoors, lay out the offerings, and make a simple prayer similar to the following:

Oh elvish spirits of the land, come forth and partake of this feast.
Dryadic beings of the woods, Gnomes of the earth
Sky-dancing Sylphs and Watery Undines
All beings of the sky, underworld, and horizon
Come forth and partake of this feast.
I offer you gratitude and respect.

Let them come and partake of the offering. During this time you can sing, meditate, drum, and of course eat and drink some food yourself. Try to perceive the spirits and relate to a few individually. At the end you can issue a dismissal that lets them know the feast is over and that you will be cleaning up. The difference with this dismissal is that you will be inviting one spirit to stay and take you as a lover and teacher:

Honored guests, the window of our communion is closing and our feast is coming to an end.
Those of you who wish to go back to your abodes and habitations
Please take your last taste of these enjoyments and go in peace.
And please forever act as friends and helpers.
If, however, you wish to stay with me, to be a lover and a teacher
That our mating may bring me further into your world
And you further into mine
Please stay. Make yourself known how you can.

From that point on whatever you experience must be your guide. Your own gifts, the gifts of the spirit being, and the willingness of it to participate will dictate what occurs. You may have a very physical sex experience as Hallgrímsdóttir reports. You may have a dream experience such as described in the last section. You may have no experience at all. I cannot say. What I can say is that just as with human relations, having sex with otherworldly beings can be dangerous. Whereas with humans, you at least have the police to call if things get obsessive or turn to assault, with spiritual beings you have only yourself or a hired sorcerer to turn to. Before attempting the work, you should be absolutely confident in your ability to banish unwanted spirits, even those that have a firm foothold in your life because you invited them. If you do not have such confidence, I would strongly recommend not inviting a demon, elf, or any other spirit into your sex life.

Of course, humans have not only been known to have sexual relations with demons, ghosts, and spirits, but also with beings such as angels and gods, who, in theory at least, exist on a higher plane than we do.

Sex with Gods

There is no shortage of examples of gods having sex with humans, often giving birth to superhuman children that change the face of human history. Greek and Roman myths are filled with god–mortal matings. Zeus comes to mind as the one who has probably bedded the most human women, fathering literally dozens of notable demigods such as Herakles, Perseus, Minos, Argos, and Alexander the Great. Gilgamesh was the son of a king and the Goddess Ninsun. And we should not forget that Jesus, the offspring of the monotheistic God and Mary, also falls into this category

In most cases sex with gods is a matter of the god choosing you rather than the other way around. There are exceptions, though. In the Mahabharata we learn that Queen Kunti was in possession of a mantra that would force a god to have sex with her and grant her a child. When her husband was cursed to die if he ever had sex again, she used the mantra to coerce Surya, Yama, Vayu, and Indra to each impregnate her with a child, leading to the birth of Karna,

Yudishtira, Bhima, and Arjuna, respectively. Arjuna, of course, along with Krishna, goes on to be one of the heroes of the Mahabharata. Sadly I don't know the mantra, so I cannot pass it on to you here.

In a sense, whenever you have sex with someone who has successfully invoked a god into him- or herself, as we discussed back in Chapter 6, you are having sex with a god. Beyond that, I don't know of any methods for having sex with Pagan gods directly, other than perhaps inviting them during prayer.

Inappropriately Touched by an Angel

Some occultists have compared the gods of Paganism with the angels of monotheistic religions, and claimed them to be similar types of beings. I don't know about that, but I do know that you don't need to look far to find angels having sex with humans. Just six chapters into Genesis you get this: "When human beings began to increase in number on the earth and daughters were born to them, the sons of God saw that the daughters of humans were beautiful, and they married any of them they chose." (Genesis 6:2-1 NIV) This story is fleshed out in the Book of Enoch quite a bit, with information on what each of the Watchers taught to mankind, and the punishments they received from God. The idea of there being a Sangreal (Holy Grail) Bloodline connected to the Nephilim is sometimes espoused by occultists. This is also the origin of the Witchblood in some traditions of Witchcraft and Cunning Arts in Europe. Some believe that all people who have the ability to practice magic are descendants of the Nephilim. Fast-forward to the late 19th century and we again have a very public example of angel-human relations, this time with a groundbreaking feminist by the name of Ida Craddock.

Ida Craddock was raised in Philadelphia as a Quaker, and was the first female ever admitted to the University of Pennsylvania, before the Board of Trustees blocked her entrance. She made her primary living by writing textbooks and teaching stenography at Girard College. In her 30s she joined the Theosophical Society and the Unitarian Church, and took an interest in occultism and yoga.

Eventually she relocated to Chicago, where, in 1893, she attended a belly-dancing exhibition at the world's fair. This dance was considered lewd by the prudish standards of the day and a movement was begun to shut it down. Craddock wrote an open letter defending the dance, suggesting that not only should it be allowed at the world's fair, but that it should be seen all across the country as a "prenuptial educator of our children." She further noted that the dance "trains the muscles of the woman in the endurance desirable in the wife...and therefore increases her capacity, not only for receiving but also for conferring pleasure."[5]

Craddock believed that fear of and disgust for sex, as well as ignorance of proper sexual technique, was a leading cause of many of society's problems. The moral societies at the time, such as the Society for the Suppression of Vice led by Anthony Comstock, did not feel the same way. Part of their attack on Craddock was to say that she was herself clearly immoral because she was not married but clearly had firsthand knowledge of sex. Ida Craddock responded that she *was* married—to an angel.

This was not married in the way that a nun is "married" to the Church. This was married in the sense that they had sex. From her diary, on October 11, 1894: "Last night, Soph and I united, mainly at the clitoris, where his organ was for a great part of the time strongly perceptible in its texture...."[6] In fact, her sexual exploits with this angel, whom she called Soph, were reportedly so loud that the neighbors complained on several occasions. Craddock went on to write more about the love between angels and humans in her book *Heavenly Bridegrooms*. She detailed a system of sex mysticism in *Psychic Wedlock*, and also wrote several other treatises on sex and female rights such as "Right Marital Living" and "The Wedding Night."

Eventually Craddock fell afoul of Comstock again, and he had her arrested for sending indecent material through the mail. Rather than serve her sentence of hard labor, she committed suicide, leaving behind a public letter defending her works, and pleading that they be protected from Comstock and others like him that would destroy them.

In her works Craddock shared a three-grade system of sex practice that was taught to her by Soph. She defines the First Degree as "sex union forbidden, except for the express purpose of creating a child." The object here is to learn self-control. The Second Degree is "sex union enjoined in absolute self-control and aspiration to the highest." Here we have instructions to have sex without orgasm, but without much of the technical advice on how to do that, such as we see in tantric and Taoist literature. The Third Degree is "Communion with Deity as the third partner in marital union."[7]

These three degrees are mirrored in the teachings of Louis Culling's Greater Brotherhood of God (GBG) as well as in the teachings of Otoman Zar-Adusht Ha'nish, but largely without credit given to where they came from. In Culling's system, in the third degree you see your physical partner as your own Holy Guardian Angel (HGA), the being spoken of extensively in the "Book of Abramelin," an important grimoire in Thelema, which advocates an 18-month process for attaining the knowledge of and conversation with this Angel.[8] It is entirely possible that Soph was Ida Craddock's HGA. Many people who have attained knowledge of and conversation with the Holy Guardian Angel, myself included, have experienced sexualized content with the angel, if not physical sex itself. Aaron Leitch, author of *Secrets of the Magical Grimoires*, pointed out in a recent blog post that the "knowledge" part of "knowledge and conversation" implies carnal knowledge. Aaron too has had sexual experiences with his HGA, whom he refers to as his Spiritual Wife.

Speaking for myself, this type of sexualized experience—I hesitate to call it actual sex—with the Holy Guardian Angel is the basis for much exchange. Just as with the angels described in Genesis 6, we receive knowledge of hidden things from the heavenly realms, and the angels receive carnal contact that is usually outside the realm of what they can experience.

One thing is clear about all these stories of men and spirits having sex (apart from the fact that we desperately need a Law and Order: Supernatural SVU) is that it is a two-way street. This is an area of magic where there can be no clear, step-by-step instructions, because it relies upon the input from at least two beings to make it happen. Because of this unknown factor of the other being we must proceed with care. Just as with human partners, they can be parasitic, obsessive, and dangerous if we let them.

CHAPTER 11

A *Different Kind of Spellbinding:*
The Sorcery of BDSM

Beyond the world of straightforward, vanilla sex lies a realm of fetishes and kinks too numerous for us to tackle in this book: foot fetishes, enemas, blood fetishes, amputees...the list is endless. One area, however, stands out as both being popular enough with general readership to warrant coverage and having significant application in the practice of sexual sorcery: BDSM.

BDSM is an initialism that stands for Bondage and Discipline, Dominance and Submission, and Sadism and Masochism. It incorporates elements of pain, restriction, roleplay, surrender, and a host of other activities. If you really don't already know what I am talking about, put the book down and go read the Wikipedia entry on BDSM. But chances are you *do* know what I am talking about.

A recent British study has found that two thirds of women have experimented with bondage and spanking. Previously something that would only be spoken of in whispers and practiced with equipment that gets well-hidden in the back of the closet, the publication of the Fifty Shades trilogy has shoved BDSM front and center into popular awareness. Business Insider reported that in 2012, hardware stores were reporting dramatically increased sales of rope— so much so that companies could not keep up supply and caused a minor shortage.[1]

People who practice BDSM range from people who live out a 24/7 Dominant–Submissive or Master–Slave lifestyle, who have dedicated entire rooms in their homes and thousands of dollars of equipment to the practice, to people who simply like to tie each other up to the bed with a necktie or silk scarf every now and then. If you choose to embark on it, as with any of the practices in this book, I only ask that you do your research, stay safe, and make sure that everything is consensual.

Popularity is not the only reason for its inclusion in this book. Many of the practices of BDSM have direct impact on the practice of magic. It is a field on which we can easily find guidance by looking to past tradition, and look to break new ground with future experiments. Think of the bound and hoodwinked candidate during Masonic and craft initiations. Think of the mystic's submission to the divine. Think of the effect that pain and sensory deprivation have on the psyche. There is much for the sorcerer to explore.

Is It Healthy?

Despite its popularity, many people question whether the desire to be held in bondage and whipped, or to do that to others, is a sign of a healthy psyche. Because we are attempting to create a healthy body and mind with sex magic, and ascend spiritually to new heights, this is a fair question to ask. Certainly in the past this and most fetishes were classified as mental disorders. Today, modern psychology tends to distinguish between paraphilia (atypical sexual interest) and a paraphilic disorder that causes distress or impairment in functioning. The DSM-5 (Diagnostic and Statistical Manual of Mental Disorders, 5th Edition) does not label BDSM a disorder unless it causes harm to the practitioner or others—this harm does not include whip marks and the occasional rope burn, of course.

Far from being unhealthy, a new study, published May 16 in the Journal of Sexual Medicine, finds that BDSM practitioners may be experiencing *better* psychological health than the average person.[2] Experts believe this to be because they are more extroverted, open to new experiences, and have more clearly established relationship parameters.

Gender, Dominance, and Submission

I spoke a bit about gender roles in the Introduction to the book, but want to revisit it in this context. Many traditional tantric and Taoist manuals talk about the man in terms of being the active principal and the woman in terms of being the passive principal. For this, and of course other patriarchal reasons, some have suggested that women are more naturally suited to, and should therefore take, the submissive role, while men should be the dominants. This is utter bunk, and wherever tradition insists upon it I am not afraid to call that tradition wrong. In Shakti Tantra, it is the woman who is the active principal whereas the man is the passive principal. Given the amount of men who pay to visit dominatrices and women who fill those roles as a profession, a lifestyle, or both, I think we can safely say there is no default setting.

There is nothing wrong with women taking the submissive role and men taking the dominant role, either during a scene or as a lifestyle. It must, however, be something that both people decide for themselves and not something they get railroaded into because a group, text, or even an entire religion tells them it is their natural state. Furthermore, these roles have nothing to do with one person being weak and another person being strong. It takes an enormous amount of strength for a man to set aside what some would see as his natural role and act or live as a submissive as his heart desires. It also takes a massive amount of strength for a woman to do the same thing: she will be accused by some of setting feminism back, or of being brainwashed, or any kind of nonsense. It is all about freedom of choice, including the choice to grant another person a dominant role over you, if that is what you truly desire—be it for the length of a few hours, or for a lifestyle. Whatever you do as a sorcerer or sorceress should be a manifestation of your strength, even if that means being locked into a collar and chains.

Safety and Safe Words

I spoke a bit about consent in the chapter on dangers, but considering we are talking about things like bondage, which will effectively place someone in a helpless situation, and whipping, which could potentially cause real damage to a person, I think revisiting it specifically in this context is a good idea.

In this day and age clear consent should be sought for all sexual encounters of any kind, but certainly in BDSM encounters extra clarity not only on consent but on limits, agreed parameters, and ways of withdrawing consent must be made absolutely clear. To borrow a phrase from a friend of mine: it should go without saying that nothing should go without saying.

Safe words are used in BDSM to establish when consent is being withdrawn. Certainly "no" and "stop" can be the words that end play, but sometimes the submissive partner (or the "sub") will like to roleplay or just be able to say those words without actually stopping the play, so out-of-context words like "Philadelphia" are used. Sometimes people use a system of words to indicate when they are getting near their limits, when they want the person to stop what they are doing but not end the scene, and when they want the scene to completely stop. If gags, hoods, or other items that would prevent speech are used, then a body sign such as shaking head three times and grunting three times loudly should be established.

Apart from this you should have some basic knowledge of what you are doing and whether it is safe or not. A book like this is really not the place to go through every detail of things like knots for safe bondage, areas of the body that you can and cannot whip, and so on. If you are serious about it you should read at least one book on the subject that is devoted entirely to BDSM.[3] What I will say is that although silk scarves and neckties may seem more innocent and less intimidating than padded leather cuffs that attach to eyehooks on the bed frame, the former is much more dangerous in terms of cutting off circulation and being impossible to get off without scissors. By all means, for casual play or introducing a lover to it, go with light and fun household items, but of you are bringing a submissive into trance, or using a whip to excite the rise of Kundalini, you should consider solid equipment.

Sensory Deprivation and Scrying

In the chapter on mind and energy we discussed the orgasm as a gateway into a state of mind useful for divination and out-of-body experience. In the chapter on spirits we saw again how this state can be used to establish communication with the spirit that has been summoned. In both cases the energy of the seer is heightened by the Inner Fire practice, which activates all their centers and causes the descending bliss—this itself often leads to visionary experiences. When orgasm is reached after a significant amount of time, the ego-shattering effect propels the mind past dualistic conception, and as it falls back into ordinary perception, thoughts, sounds, and images may arise that relate to the subject of the rite. Experienced practitioners who have gained competency in astral projection will find that they can sometimes launch out of their body during this process.

To aid in shutting out distractions and dwelling deeper in the inner worlds that open up in states like this, yogis sometimes use a technique called the Yoni Mudra to shut out the senses. The ears are covered with the thumbs, index fingers cover the eyes, middle fingers pinch the nostrils, and lips are held tight by clamping them between the ring and pinkie finger. This is traditional. A little bondage gear can achieve an even greater effect to this end than the Yoni Mudra: a blindfold for the eyes, earplugs for the ears, and perhaps a harness gag for the mouth. The only thing missing is the clamp over the nose, which I have found doesn't add much to the experience anyway. You can also use a bondage hood that will cover the entire head in leather, with only holes to breathe through.

Binding the limbs can also increase this feeling of being removed from the world. Most people placed into strict but comfortable bondage that does not place undue stress on the body will stop struggling or testing their bonds after a few minutes and instead focus on other senses. As each of these senses get blocked, more and more attention is drawn to the inner world. For those who want to take this work to an extreme there is the famous "Witches' Cradle." This was a sort of sling used as a torture device during the Inquisition, in which a suspect is essentially mummified in a covering, strapped onto a frame, and suspended in the air so that she would spin and lose all sense of up, down, left, and right. Modern witches have adopted it into the craft, and it has been mentioned in Raymond Buckland's *Complete Book of Witchcraft* and Donald Michael Kraig's *Modern Sex Magick*. Short of a sensory deprivation tank, it is about as far as you can go in cultivating a sense of shutting out physical senses.

If you are planning on doing the cradle, or some variation of it, make sure that you attach it to eyebolts that are firmly anchored in a beam—that hook for your plants that you put in with a wall anchor is not going to cut it. Make sure that you also have safe equipment that does not place unnecessary stress on the body, and ensure the ability to breathe. If you want to incorporate suspension but not go as far as the full Witches' Cradle, make sure you use proper suspension cuffs or a harness purchased from a good supplier. Dangling people from handcuffs is for movies *only*. Again, I strongly recommend books and classes that are specifically about BDSM technique and safety.

All of this is dependent on being someone who is comfortable and calm in bondage. I want to caution people who do not enjoy bondage and sensory deprivation against using this technique; it will not yield good results for you. Also, if you are person who likes bondage, but enjoys the struggle or play-acting of a rape scenario,[4] this is not a good choice for you either. Such activities are fine for the bedroom (and psychology today reports that 31 to 57 percent of women are excited by rape fantasies[5]), but this is not the fulcrum on which this sorcery operates. Scrying demands a movement away from normal physical senses, and a movement to inner and subtle senses. If the bondage does not facilitate this, it can still be fun, but not useful for this type of work.

Never let the sex overshadow the work, nor the work overshadow the sex. Harmony and integration of the two are the key to the success of everything in this book.

Bondage and Edging

Throughout the book I have been advocating prolonged sex as necessary for successful sorcery. Physical methods such as the lower lock as well as changing pace and thrust have all played a part in this. Bondage can also be used to achieve this end, but it requires your partner to be able to recognize all the signs of an impending orgasm.

This is called edging: bringing someone to the edge of orgasm, then backing off and bringing them back to the edge again and again. It is a sort of pleasurable torture in BDSM, but also a useful technique for prolonging sex play for creating the Elixir or for internal energetic work. The bondage element is needed simply to stop the recipient of these attentions, usually the man, from just finishing himself off. The recipient is forced to channel that frustrated energy back into the Inner Fire and circulate it throughout his body. His orgasm will finally come when the dominant decides it is time.

This also has uses in Eroto-Comatose Lucidity. I am sure if you go back and read the section again you can see how bondage can aid the comatose state, and blindfolds, hoods, and earplugs can add to the lucidity.

Whipping and Scourging

Did you know that the Kama Sutra has a section on spanking? Comparing lovemaking to a quarrel that gets more and more heated, it recommends that "striking" be used to drive it to a climactic point. The actual advice of the Kama Sutra on where and how is a little violent and includes fists to the back, chops to the head, and other moves that might be more than your average person wants to experience. This love manual was written sometime between 400 BC and AD 200, showing that mixing pleasure and pain in the bedroom is nothing new.

Apart from purely pleasurable purposes, striking and flagellation have been used from time immemorial as a means of purification and penance as well as a method of achieving higher states of consciousness. Monks and members of Opus Dei have been known to whip themselves as a way of identifying with the passion of Christ. Members of the Luperci or brotherhood of the wolf would run through the streets of ancient Rome whipping people as a blessing. Women would line up to receive the blows, which were thought to transfer the blessings of fertility with them. In certain initiatory traditions of Wicca, priests and priestesses take turns binding and scourging each other in order to excite the witch-power that lies dormant in the body.

A study at Northern Illinois University recently found that during sadomasochistic play in which pain is administered, blood flows away from the dorsolateral and prefrontal cortex, which are responsible in part for distinguishing self from other, which leads the participant to a sense of oneness that is often described as spiritual and liberating.[6] Indeed, this feeling and brain reaction is similar to what happens during meditation. It is very interesting to note that these changes happen not only in people receiving pain but for people who administer it as well. Hard materialists will look at this activity in the brain and treat it as the sole explanation for the effect and use it to discount any kind of spiritual contact or mystical benefit. To these people I would say that your brain reacts a certain way when you encounter a cheese sandwich as well. This is not evidence that there is no such thing as cheese sandwiches. The physical brain and body are just as important to spirituality and magic as the subtle bodies are. In sexual magic they play an even greater role.

If you do decide to incorporate whipping into your magic as a way of reaching altered states, be it for vision work, communicating with spirits, or as a method of charging those sigils we have been talking about, make sure that you do it safely.

Many people note that whipping further stimulates Inner Heat and Kundalini, which is true, but you must not attempt to stimulate the fire at the navel chakra directly. In both the front and back of the body you have too many organs unprotected by bones and significant muscle. Focus on the buttocks or a light whipping of the genitals while the person receiving the whipping raises the seed there to strike the navel chakra, starting the fire. As the fire ascends you can focus on the upper back and chest.

Apart from where you hit, you should know what you are hitting with and how it feels, whether it's a flogger, a crop, or spanking with your hand.

Breath Play

I hesitate to even include this in the book, as it is *very* dangerous, but yet another way to create altered states of consciousness is breath play: the restriction of oxygen. This is usually done with nose pinching, choking with the hands, or in some cases smothering with the dominant partner's body parts. You can also use gas masks and special hoods made for this purpose.

This play is also not entirely new to the world of sorcery. Russian Occultist Maria De Naglowska, who in 1932 established the Confrerie de la Flèche d'Or, or Brotherhood of the Golden Arrow, in Paris, taught a rite that incorporated ritual hanging as an ordeal of the Brotherhood. Candidates knew full well that there was a possibility that they might not survive the ordeal, but chose to undergo it anyway because of the gnosis that it supposedly produced. Naglowska writes, "At the moment nothing any longer calls the things of daily life to the mind of the one tested, he has the clear impression of suddenly finding himself face to face with what could very improperly be called the Infinite."[7]

I am not going to discuss how to perform this type of activity because, in my opinion, there is no vision or state that it could possibly produce that would be worth the risk. Hundreds of people die every year from breath play, either alone or with a partner. The most famous recent example would be David Carradine, star of the *Kung Fu* television series and Kill Bill movies, who was found hanging by a rope in a closet of his hotel room in Thailand. The coroner concluded that it was most likely auto-erotic asphyxiation. My only reason for even covering it in the book is that it has played a part in the history of sex magic. Not everything that is traditional is a good idea, though, and this is a practice that I strongly advise against unless you are an expert in the practice already.

The Pairing of Gods and Mortals

In the chapter on invocation I focused on the union of two people who were seeing themselves as divine: both either taking on the role of gods or unlocking their own divine nature through meditation and divine pride. But this is not the only possibility. In the last chapter we took a look at the union of gods, angels, fairies, and demons with mortals, and the ways in which this gave the spirit or deity a chance to manifest its presence on the material plane, and a chance for the mortal to be uplifted by service to the deity. In dominance and submission this can play itself out by having the dominant perform the invocation and hold the presence, or even be possessed by, the deity in question. The submissive in turn will submit to the will of the god, and worship him or her as the god demands. This can include sex, of course, but also other types of service and suffering.

Many sorcerers and sorceresses these days balk at the idea of submission to the divine and bristle against Christian prayers proclaiming the unworthiness of the servant and willingness to submit to the will of the Lord, but truth be told there is deep magic here. These statements and actions place the ego aside and leave space for the divine nature to shine through. I am reminded of the prayer of St. Joseph the Visionary that is still repeated by some Greek seers before divining the future:

Cleanse my hidden mind with the hyssop of your grace
For I draw near to the holy of holies of your mysteries
Wash me from all my understanding of the flesh
and may an understanding of the spirit be mingled with my soul
Cause to reside in me a faith that perceives your mysteries,
so that I may perceive you as you are, and not as I am.
Create in me eyes that I may see with your eyes,
what I cannot see with my own
May every bodily image be wiped from my mind's eye
and may you alone be recognized before the eye of the mind.
Amen.

Many submissives enter a state they call "sub-space," a trance state that is often described as floating in your own mind. This state is a spiritual experience very close or identical to that reached by religious dedicants who consume their whole being with the will of their chosen deity. I am sure some readers will disagree and even be upset that I am comparing a state of being reached by a dedicated nun with a state reached by someone having kinky sex, but I am not the first to do so.

The idea of one person taking the role of a humble worshipper and another taking the role of a god or goddess is not foreign to tradition, either. In the Yoni Tantra and other Shakti Tantric texts, Yogis are instructed to worship at the altar of women and treat them as the goddess herself. The woman playing this role can be their wives, their guru's wives, and in some texts even sisters, daughters, and grandmothers. While such acts would be criminal in our society—and for that matter in India as well—the idea of worshipping a living person as the god is not new.

In BDSM spiritual practice this might take the form of the submissive being placed in bondage and blindfolded, similar to a hoodwinked candidate at a Masonic or witchcraft initiation. This could be followed by the dominant performing an invocation and allowing the hod to merge with him or her, or unveil his or her divine pride. The dominant, now "ridden" by the god, can instruct the submissive in whatever acts of worship, penance, or service he or she desires. Even something that the submissive may not enjoy for his or her own pleasure might be used to deepen the sense of submission. I am often told that the joy a submissive receives is in doing things he or she might not otherwise enjoy, but knowing that his or her dominant does. This could be anything from whipping or sex play to simply waiting in bondage for release. The precise details of what occurs will be up to the three-way relationship of sub, dom, and deity.

At the end of the service, the god can release the aspirant from all bondage and sense-deprivation, symbolizing the new state of freedom and true perception that he or she has achieved, again very similar to what occurs in an initiation rite.

My one warning here is that partners should trust each other as dominant and submissive before they enter divine service into it. The list of gurus and living gods who have coerced or threatened people into submission is long, and doing so leads to no good end. If you suspect someone will abuse the power you have handed to him or her as a dominant, do not add a god complex to the mix!

Human Sacrifice

You know the scene. The sorcerer is robed and holding a candle and spell book over the writhing body of a beautiful virgin chained to the altar.[8] He is summoning up an elder god or demon, but before he can perform the sacrifice, or before the monster eats the young virgin, the hero sweeps in and saves the day. What if, though, instead of the hero coming in, the sorcerer completes the ritual, but the sacrifice turns out not to cost the young virgin her life? In fact, it turns out she was a willing and eager participant all along.

Sacrifice can take many forms. Sometimes offerings of food and incense are referred to as sacrifices. Sometimes people give up doing certain things they enjoy as a sacrifice. Sometimes people surrender important items, and sometimes people endure pain or discomfort as a sacrifice to the gods.

If you have ever attended an animal sacrifice such as is practiced in many traditional religions, you notice something: The gods do not actually lap up the physical blood. When I went to the sacrifices to Kali at DakshinKali in Nepal, the floor of the outdoor temple was covered, ankle high, in blood from all the animals that had given their lives to Kali, and whose meat was later cooked and eaten. Kali was clearly drawing something more subtle from the blood, something that could perhaps be provided in a different way.[9]

In the last chapter I spoke a bit about offering the energy of sex or the fluids produced from sex to spirits. You can carry the whole act further with a submissive who is willing to trade his or her pain, comfort, and vital essence in exchange for visions and power from the spirit.

As I said in before, not every spirit would be interested in such a sacrifice, but those that are tend to consider this energy released from pain/pleasure a very good offering. Gods of intellect and healing might not enjoy such a display, but a god of war, a chthonic entity, or a wrathful guardian would be able to draw much sustenance from the force released by a bound sacrifice who was undergoing a flogging and/or other sensual tortures. Such a person could be placed with a scrying device before him or her, or hoodwinked so that he or she could act as both seer and sacrifice simultaneously.

You might also choose to be bound in sacrifice in a more traditional manner and allow the spirits to feed off you directly. In his chapbook "Waters of Return: The Aeonic Flow of Voudoo," Louis Martine describes a ritual called the Spider Rite that is aimed at gaining familiars, or personal working spirits, through feeding them your own essence.[10] In the rite the celebrant is chained in the middle of the temple with a Veve[11] shaped like a web drawn on his or her chest. Veves of the four Spider Loa are drawn at the cross quarters, North West, North East, South-West, South-East, and lines of cornmeal are made leading from the spider Veves to the web Veve on the sorcerer's chest. Four assistants summon the Spider Loa by drumming in a style suited to the Petro Loa, emphasizing off-beats, and then leave the room. Left alone, the spiders feed on the sorcerer's essence, and in the process become weighed down with his will. The sorcerer will now be linked to these Spider Loa and be able to enter their minds and travel in their astral forms, navigating the vast web that is spun between all living beings, through all times and all dimensions. At the end of the rite he or she is released, and the cornmeal and remains of the Veves are presented to the celebrant.

This rite would need to be performed by people who are rock solid in their will and power, lest they find themselves in the grip of the very thing they fed. Though you may not always do it in an attempt to gain a familiar, such a sacrifice can earn you much reward from the right kind of spirit. The wrong kind of spirit, though, will either be offended or take advantage of the situation to obsess and control the sacrifice.

I know of someone who has a very large version of the triangle of manifestation from the Goetia. They have wrist shackles at the apex and a leg-cuff on each of the lower points so that a sacrifice and seer may be fed on and possessed by the demon evoked into the triangle. This is not something I would try or recommend, but neither he nor his significant other seem to have suffered any ill effects from being chained within.

Not for Everyone

The rites discussed in this chapter are not for everyone. They are not *necessary* to sex magic in any way. It is a fact, though, that many people involved in magic, Paganism, and the occult are also practitioners of BDSM. It is also a fact that practitioners of BDSM report spiritual and mystical experiences during their play. As with any type of sexual activity, let those who find it distasteful move on. Let those who are interested pursue it in a way that is safe, sane, and consensual.

4 Rites of Sexual Sorcery

Throughout the book I have presented exercises and techniques largely without the context of tradition or ritual structure. This is so that the focus is squarely on where it needs to be for this work: mastering techniques rather than memorizing rituals. Spells and rituals are wonderful, but sometimes I feel as though people become focused too tightly on finding more and more rituals, and of course the leather-bound tomes that contain them, than they are on actually training in the art. The latest-received text or the newest translation of an obscure grimoire will not provide you with some key that has been utterly lacking in your magic up to this point—only actual work will do that. People who put the exercises of this book into practice will become people of power rather than people who know lots of arcane bits and pieces.

That said, it can be helpful to put these practices into a ritual context with specific symbols, god forms, and so on. You should feel free to use the following rituals as they are presented, or use them as ideas for creating your own. Remember, most of the techniques in this book do not need to be performed according to a ritual script. The primary importance is to develop competency and mastery in the methods I have presented. Without competence in those methods and the abilities of concentration, stamina, control, and etheric-body development that they provide, the performance of the following rituals will be an empty exercise.

Rite of Harmonia

This ritual is a work on internal alchemy that transforms the passions of wrath and lust into the wisdom of harmony.

Step 1: The male and female components of the rite should enter the temple, with the male clothed in a red robe or toga, and the female attired in a light-green or golden robe or toga.

Step 2: Enter into meditation and see your own body dissipate into space. Rest in this state of emptiness.

Step 3: Arise as the symbol of the invoked gods. In this case you can arise as Aphrodite and Ares and see these symbols representing them:

Imagine that this symbol sends out light in all directions, and that this light reflects back upon you, forming the stainless body of the Aphrodite or Ares (depending upon which role your are playing). This symbol arises at your heart, your very essential center.

Step 4: Let the male invoke the god Ares thusly:

Ares, boisterous and brave in battle!

Strict and Severe Sovereign Soldier

Fill me with your ruthless resolve

Enflame me with Fierceness and Force

Let me burn bright with holy rage

And desire for conquest!

Step 5: Let the female invoke the goddess Aphrodite:

Aphrodite, beautiful and fair!

Damsel of Delicious Delight

Bathe me in your golden Green Grace

Let your Passion Possess me

Let your Lust Liberate me

And your desire drive me on!

Note: Steps 5 and 6 can be switched if desired. You should repeat the conjurations, chant the names, and keep intensely inviting the presence of the deity to manifest in the astral form that you have provided. When you feel the presence, you may proceed.

Step 6: As the deity, perform the Inner Fire technique. As the fire rises, and you become more subtle, the divine presence will take further hold. When the dripping and blazing starts, move to Step 7.

Step 7: Let Aphrodite approach Ares and remove his red robes and say,

My God of War and Wrath

Arise and Awaken to my Adorations.

Let Aphrodite kiss and suckle his perineum and penis as Ares blazes the Inner Fire. Aphrodite says,

I stir thee and summon thee forth.

Let Aphrodite kiss his chest over his heart center as Ares circulates the flames at his heart, melting the drop. Aphrodite continues,

To embrace me and fill me.

Let Aphrodite kiss Ares' throat as he circulates the flames in his throat center, melting the drop. Aphrodite continues,

To speak my holy name in the throes of passion.

Let Aphrodite kiss Ares' head as he circulates the flames in his crown, melting the drop. Aphrodite continues,

To let my lust transform your wrath into ecstasy.

Step 8: Let Ares remove Aphrodite's robes, saying,

My Goddess of Love and Lust

Open yourself to my worship of you.

Let Ares kiss and suckle her vagina and clitoris as Aphrodite blazes the Inner Fire. Ares says,

I stir thee and summon thee forth.

Let Ares kiss Aphrodite's chest over her heart center as she circulates the flames at her heart, melting the drop. Ares says,

To embrace me and be filled by me.

Let Ares kiss Aphrodite's throat as she circulates the flames in her throat center, melting the drop. Ares continues,

To speak my holy name in the throes of passion.

Let Ares kiss Aphrodite's head as she circulates the flames in her crown, melting the drop. Ares continues,

To let our passions join and transform into ecstasy.

Step 9: Let Ares and Aphrodite join in sex. Keep the inner fires burning. Keep the mind focused on the divine pride of the deity. Keep the passions excited.

There is no need to stay in one position, or perform only one act. Alternating between positions, or switching between occasional oral sex and intercourse can be done with no problem. Stimulation need not be mutual at all times; it is okay for one person to pleasure the other for a few minutes and for that person to relax and be receptive. Continue to worship each other for at least 20 minutes before moving to the next Step.

Step 10: Choose one position that you can maintain for 10 to 15 minutes or so. Focus back on the sigil at your heart. Let Ares make his sigil descend, and send his sigil into Aphrodite through the penis. At the same time let Aphrodite make her sigil ascend through her mouth into the mouth of Ares. Let the symbols form a loop through the central channel, each chasing the other as they pass from mouth to genitals again and again. You can reverse this direction if it feels more natural.

Step 11: Lose yourself to the ecstasy and let the symbols merge. This does not have to form a complex sigil that you can draw; it is the feel and sensation that is important here. You can, if you like, simply see them melding into a sphere. This is the creation of Harmonia—Harmonia being the child of Ares and Aphrodite in myth. In this ritual it represents the passions blown to cosmic levels, united and transformed. Keep this flowing until the moment of release.

Step 12: When orgasm comes, you should strive to make it simultaneous. If not, then both parties must eventually orgasm. During the moment of release, both parties (even if one is not orgasming at this moment) should be sure to perform the lower lock or the Vajroli technique. The male should orgasm, but not ejaculate. Through the Inner Fire, breaths, and locks, the energy from the release is sent up the central channel into the higher centers of both people, shattering whatever is left of identifying as either their normal egos or as Ares and Aphrodite.

Step 13: Let the energy circulate. Release any pretense of invocation and land gently back to your own selves. Continue to embrace as this occurs.

Step 14: Thank and dismiss the powers. Make offerings and close the temple. Say,

Ares and Aphrodite, thank you for your passion and power

You have honored us with your presence

Let us honor you with gifts and glory.

All other beings attracted by this rite, be released.

Go in peace.

Simple Sigil of Mercury

Step 1: On a Wednesday create a simple sigil representing your goal: In this example it will be to find the perfect place to live as a couple. You can create a sigil using any method, but in this case let's use the typical letter-merging method. First we create a sentence to represent the desire: TO FIND A NEAR PERFECT PLACE FOR US TO LIVE. Cross out the repeating letters so you are left with this string: TOFINDANERPCLUSV. Spend some time combing them into an attractive and suitably arcane-looking symbol:

Note that this symbol not only has all the letters within it, but it also recalls the astrological symbol for Mercury, making it doubly effective.

Step 2: At the hour of Mercury, paint the sigil on each other's bodies in fluorescent orange body paint. Paint it at least eight times on each person: the forehead, the throat, the chest, below the navel, the upper back, lower back, and the backs of the hands. Rather than candles you can light the chamber with black lights so that the sigils glow brightly.

Step 3: Invoke Hermes or Mercury for your desired outcome and dedicate the rite to him. Say,

Honorable and Holy Hermes

Swift and Skillful Sage

We dedicate this rite to your honor and glory

We pray that you find it pleasing

Please bless us, and this seal,

Which carries our will

To find a new home.

When we find this home

We will again honor you

And sing your praises publicly.

Step 4: Perform the Inner Fire technique up to the blazing and dripping.

Step 5: Begin sexual union. Keep the Inner Fires burning. Keep the mind focused on the sigils. They are painted all over your bodies, so seeing the sigil should not be a problem no matter what position or sexual method you use.

Step 6: At the moment of release, make sure that your entire attention is drawn to the sigil. Let your eyes rest upon it as you shatter forth, and reassemble after the moment. If orgasm is not simultaneous, make sure that both people orgasm while looking at the seal.

Step 7: After both of you have had your release, wash the seals off one another and give a general dismissal and closing.

The Bounty of Zeus and Demeter

This ritual is done for empowering a Jupiter glyph or other talisman designed to increase business. (More on gyph talismans can be found in my book *Financial Sorcery*.)

Step 1: Prepare a parchment with glyphs to support your financial goal. For this spell we will use the example of starting a new business. We might choose these glyphs: Viral Marketing, Entrepreneurial Success, Steady Work, and Defeating Competition (shown here clockwise from upper left).

Step 2: The male invokes Zeus, saying,

Oh Zeus, Supreme Sovereign

Whose laughter unleashes lightning and life itself!

Who bestows bounty both boundless and blessed!

I invite you to enter me and bless me.

And to Adore and Worship your lover Demeter.

Step 3: The female invokes Demeter, saying,

Oh Demeter, Goddess of Growth

Benevolent, Blessed, and Bountiful.

Who rewards wise planting with plentiful harvest.

I invoke you to enter me and bless me.

And to Adore and Worship your lover Zeus.

Step 4: Place the seal at the center of the place where you are to make love. Each of you make the triangle of manifestation by joining your thumbs and index finger tips. Both of you place them over the seal and entwine the rest of your fingers together. The effect should be that you are each staring at the seal through your own triangle but that your hands are linked together by the other fingers. Pray together:

Oh Father Zeus, Oh Mother Demeter

Bring your blessings upon this seal.

May the seeds planted today and through our own hard work

Bear the abundant fruit of wealth and wellbeing.

May this business be a success.

May word of it spread and attract new clients.

May clients be steady and plenty.

May competitors and enemies be defeated.

May our Success give you Glory

And benefit all.

Step 5: While still holding hands, begin the Inner Fire technique until the blazing and dripping begins.

Step 6: Enter into sexual union. Keep the Inner Fires burning. Keep the mind focused on the divine pride of the deity. Keep the passions excited. As much as possible, try to keep the seal under the point of contact. The position does not matter. Just keep the seal under the area. Make love for at least 20 minutes.

Step 7: When you reach orgasm, let the seed of Zeus release and be cultivated by the fluids of Demeter. The Elixir is the result.

Step 8: Zeus should draw out the Elixir with his tongue and share it with Demeter in a kiss. Both should apply to it the parchment with the glyphs on it, making sure each seal is individually touched and consecrated. Say,

By the Blessings of Zeus and Demeter
May this seal bring success and plenty.

Step 9: Thank and dismiss the powers. Make offerings. Close the temple.

The Vision of the Angel Lover

This ritual is aimed at gaining a vision and possibly establishing contact with your Holy Guardian Angel. The concept of the HGA is a deep one in ceremonial magic and is rooted in a text called the Book of Abramelin, which details an 18-month ritual to make contact. Aleister Crowley claimed to make contact with his HGA via Liber Samekh, and other modern magicians have done it through a variety of means.

As discussed in Chapter 10, many people have a loving or sexual relationship with their HGA. Some teach, as Ida Craddock and Louis Culling both have, that you can identify your partner with your Holy Guardian Angel. I will be honest here and say that because this is not the method I used for attaining the Knowledge and Conversation of my Holy Guardian Angel, I have no idea if this would work or not. But it certainly couldn't hurt, and failing could at least be fun.

Step 1: The Seeker is blindfolded with a black blindfold upon which is painted the words **AOTH ABRAOTH BASYM ISAK SABAOTH IAO.**

Step 2: The Seeker kneels and prays before his or her partner, who is standing:

I conjure the Graal of God, the Aeon of the Aeons

Let me prostrate myself before thee

And Submit to thy will.

Send me my angel this night.

Make me worthy to know and love her [or him; whatever the gender of your partner is]

Whereby, in beholding her

Glorifies her in this vision

Step 3: The Seeker's partner binds the Seeker to a bed in a spread-eagle position, symbolizing the openness to contact. The bonds should be comfortable: loose enough that there is no strain, but strict enough that the Seeker cannot break free or move overly much. The idea here is to get the Seeker to forget the body, not to cause him or her pain or punishment. Earplugs can also be used to block out outside noises.

Step 4: The partner anoints the head of the Seeker with oil, as the Seeker says,

The mark of majesty of Sacred Kings

and seal of sanctity on priests

is set with consecrated oil.

Please anoint me, O lord

Purify, Cleanse, and Dignify me

That I may have the vision of mine angel

And know her [or his] embrace.

Step 5: The partner begins to make love to the Seeker. Though the Seeker may have performed the Inner Fire exercise before this rite, it is not necessary or recommended that he or she do so now. Now is a time for losing oneself. The Seeker considers that it is the angel who is making love to him or her—the "knowledge" part of "Knowledge and Conversation" being knowledge in the biblical sense.

At most the Seeker should keep asking the angel to grant a vision. The best prayers are those in the Seeker's own words; prayers from the heart. If, however, those words fail, there is a particular Greek chant that has worked marvels for me:

Aposteilon

moi ton idion

angelon te nykti

Epikaloumai

se hagie angele!

The meaning is: *I call to my angel this night. I invoke you, Holy Angel.*

Step 6: The partner should remain silent through all this and try to keep the Seeker in a state of ecstasy.

Sex should continue for decent length of time, say, 30 minutes, yet not send the Seeker into frustration from teasing, unless you are using Eroto-Comatose Lucidity techniques. The session is over when the Seeker finally has an orgasm.

Step 7: At the moment of orgasm the Seeker can choose to either release fully and collapse into holy exhaustion or to retain the energy (and fluid if it is a man) and direct it to the star center above the head. One is akin to fully surrendering to the angel's presence, the other akin to rising up to meet the angel halfway. Let intuition and ability guide you.

Do Not Be a Slave to Rituals

I want to repeat again that these rituals are merely guides. You *can* do them as written, but they are really here to show the context in which some of the techniques can be placed. In almost every case the Inner Heat practice, as well as other breath techniques, will make a huge difference in success and experience. I am sure that capable sorcerers and sorceresses will be able to devise rites of their own that are applicable to their work.

Just keep in mind that not *every* spirit or tradition interfaces well with sexual magic. Many practitioners of Palo, Santeria, and other African Traditional Religions warn that sex magic of the kind we discuss here is incompatible with the spirits and mysteries that serve.

In other traditions, a being may require initiation or have a body of sexual magic connected with it already, in which case you should not attempt to use that deity with these rites unless you possess the required initiations and have received signs. In all cases let respect, caution, research, and divination be your guide.

Notes

Chapter 1

1. See *The Wine and the Will: Rabelais Bacchic Christianity* by Florence Weinberg for evidence of this inspiration.

2. The inseparability of the personal will and divine will is the deeper mystery to be explored here.

Chapter 2

1. This is the now-famous "Rule 34": if it exists, there is a porn for it.

2. See Chapter 8.

Chapter 3

1. *Astral* means "star," thus it is the Star Body.

Chapter 4

1. Kozhevnikov, Maria, James Elliott, Jennifer Shephard, and Klaus Grammann, "Neurocognitive and Somatic Components of Temperature Increases during g-Tummo Meditation: Legend and Reality." Public Library of Science (PLOS One), March 29, 2013, *www.plosone.org/ article/info%3Adoi%2F10.1371%2Fjournal.pone.0058244.*

2. Asana is a type of position for meditation. Most famous is the lotus position, but the siddhasana or half lotus is much easier to do. I don't have room in the book for a full discussion of asana, and so I leave it to you to research.

Chapter 5

1. Risher, Brittany, "You Won't Go Blind: Great excuses for your nightly date with Pamela Handerson," MensHealth.com,   *www.menshealth.com/health/health-and-sexual-benefits-masturbation.*

2. It is the seed syllable of Dzambhalla and several other wealth deities.

3. *www.runesoup.com.*

Chapter 6

1. Randolph, Paschal Beverly, *Magis Sexualis, Reprint Edition*, Inner Traditions, 2012.

2. This is a real example that someone shared with me, by the way. Life is *way* stranger than anything I can make up.

3. Rabbi Moses Cordovero, in the *Or ha-Hayyim, Azulai*.

4. This Egyptian-derived name is claimed to be Aphrodite's name in the Greek Magical Papyrii. *PGM IV.1265-74*.

5. In researching the book I was flabbergasted by how little research there is on the female orgasm. Scientists still cannot come to a consensus on whether all women ejaculate during orgasm, or even what it is that they ejaculate. Some claim it's just urine, some that it's prostate matter that ends up the bladder, and others claim it's something else entirely.

Chapter 7

1. Secret consort.

Chapter 8

1. *The Hermetic and Alchemical Writings of Paracelsus*, Martino Fine Books (September 16, 2009).

2. Agamemnon, Aeschylus, written 458 BCE, translated by E.D.A. Morshea.

3. XI* Rocket to Uranus, "Anal Intercourse and the O.T.O.," Peter-Robert Koenig *www.parareligion.ch/sunrise/xi.htm*

4. If you try this technique (I have not), make sure that there is a hole or something to release the vacuum seal, or use enough lubrication that it is not a problem.

5. *Christianity and the Roman Empire: Background Texts*, Ralph Martin Novak 2001, Bloomsbury T&T Clark.

6. The property the farm is on used to belong to Karl Germer, the former head of the Ordo Templi Orientis. Sacha Germer, his wife, is said to have spilled the ashes on a tree in an ecstatic trance or drunken stupor, depending upon who is relating the story.

7. Aleister Crowley wrote in his journal on August 8, 1923, "The Industrial use of Semen will revolutionize human society." *The Magical Diaries of Aleister Crowley*, by Aleister Crowley (author) and Steven Skinner (editor), Weiser Books, subsequent edition (February 1996).

8. "Yoga Teachers Bizarre Display," AP Archive, January 25, 2000. *www.aparchive.com/metadata/INDIA-MUMBAI-YOGA-TEACHERS-BIZARRE-DISPLAY/23f2af6ececaof3f 920ed3f940c4b1df?searchfilter=Compilations%2Fwackies %2FBest+Of+Wackies%2F19624.*

9. Mallinson, James, "Yoga and Sex: What is the Purpose of Vajrolī Mudrā?" Yoga in Transformation: Historical and Contemporary Perspectives on a Global Phenomenon, International Conference September 19–21, 2013, Vienna. *www.yogaintransformation.wissweb.at/index. php?id=1229.*

10. *The Candamaharosana Tantra*, A Critical Edition and English Translation by Christopher S. George, American Oriental Society, 1974.

11. Many thanks to Christopher Bradford for granting permission to quote this inner order document.

12. For more information on planetary hours and planetary magic, see my book *Advanced Planetary Magic*, which is available at StrategicSorcery.net.

Chapter 9

1. I am not recommending this as something you should do, but simply stating it was done by the Fraternitas Saturni in Germany. Whatever your position on mind-altering substances, considering current drug laws and harsh penalties I would strongly urge you *not* to do something like this unless it is legal where you live. It is not necessary for the work.

2. Credited with inventing the first solid rocket fuel and a principal founder of Jet Propulsion Laboratories (NASA JPL).

3. Founder of Scientology.

4. In Taoist training, the navel, where the Inner Fire is, as well as the heart and head, are referred to as Cinnabar Fields.

Chapter 10

1. Though strangely not in Greece, where the focus of Miasma was squarely on semen.

2. There are other methods, such as the WILD technique, yogas from Niguma, and the use of drugs like Melatonin

and Huperzine A that extend the halflife of neurons, but for this book the MILD technique will get you started.

3. Wilde, Lady, *Ancient Legends, Mystic Charms, and Superstitions of Ireland*, 1887. Online at SacredTexts.com: *www.sacred-texts.com/neu/celt/ali/ali015.htm*; and Pitt. edu: *www.pitt.edu/~dash/abduct.html#ethna*.

4. Available through *www.anobii.com*.

5. *Sexual Outlaw and Erotic Mystic: The Essential Ida Craddock*, Vere Chappell, Weiser Books, 2010.

6. Ibid.

7. Ibid.

8. For more on my thoughts on the HGA, see my article "9 Pieces of Heart Advice on the HGA" in the *Holy Guardian Angel* anthology, Nephilim Press, 2014.

Chapter 11

1. Bost, Callie, "Hardware Stores Are Experiencing a Boom in Rope Sales Thanks to a Certain Erotic Novel," BusinessInsider.com, June 7, 2012. *www.businessinsider. com/fifty-shades-of-grey-has-increased-rope-sales-at-hardware-stores-2012-6*.

2. *The Journal of Sexual Medicine* vol. 10, issue 8: (2013). Article first published online May 16, 2013.

3. *Screw the Roses, Send Me the Thorns: The Romance and Sexual Sorcery of Sadomasochism*, by Philip Miller and Molly Devon, is my recommendation.

4. I stress, *play acting*.

5. Michael Castman. "Women's Rape Fantasies: How Common? What Do They Mean?" *Psychology Today* (2010).

6. Ambler, J.K., E.M. Lee, K. Klement, E. Comber, S.A, Hanson, B. Cutler, N. Cutler, T. Loewald, and B.J. Sagarin. *Sadomasochism as a path to altered states of consciousness (in preparation).* (2014).

7. Naglowska, Maria De, and Donald Traxler, trans., *Advanced Sex Magic: The Hanging Mystery Initiation,* Inner Traditions, 2011.

8. My favorite scene of this type is from the 1970 film adaptation of Lovecraft's "The Dunwich Horror," starring Dean Stockwell and Sandra Dee.

9. This is exactly how Buddhist Tantrics developed Blood Red Tormas to appease beings who would ordinarily receive a sacrificed victim.

10. Black Moon Publishing, 1992.

11. A Veve is a type of ritual symbol used in Vodou to symbolize a Loa or Mysterie.

References and Resources

As I stated at the beginning of the book, this work stands upon the shoulders of giants in both Eastern and Western traditions. Following are just a few of the works on the subject that have been influential on me.

Apart from these works that are publically available I have drawn upon numerous documents that are privately circulated among Western Alchemical Orders and Tantic Initiates, as well as oral instruction from many teachers. I mention this not to tease about secret knowledge, but to encourage the seeker to get personally involved in the search and to seek out those knowledge-holders who are willing to teach.

Western Alchemy and Sex Magic

Opening the Book of the Lambspring, by Christoper Bradford (Hadean Press, November 2011)

The Book of Coelius, by Christopher Bradford (Hadean Press, November 2012)

The Complete Magick Curriculum of the Secret Order G.B.G.: Being the Entire Study, Curriculum, Magick Rituals, and Initiatory Practices of the G.B.G (The Great Brotherhood of God), by Louis T. Culling and Carl Llewellyn Weschcke (Llewellyn Publications, Exp Rev edition, August 8, 2010)

Sexual Outlaw, Erotic Mystic: The Essential Ida Craddock by Vere Chappell and Mary K. Greer (Foreword) (Weiser Books, December 1, 2010)

Magia Sexualis: Sexual Practices for Magical Power, by Paschal Beverly Randolph (author), Maria de Naglowska (author), and Donald Traxler (translator, Introduction) (Inner Traditions, August 27, 2012)

Paschal Beverly Randolph: A Nineteenth-Century Black American Spiritualist, Rosicrucian, and Sex Magician, by John Patrick Deveney (State University of New York Press, November 14, 1996)

The Secret Rituals of the O.T.O., by Francis King (CreateSpace Independent Publishing Platform, May 27, 2014)

Secrets of the German Sex Magicians: A Practical Handbook for Men and Women, by Frater U.D. (Llewellyn Publications, October 8, 1995)

Modern Magick: 11 Lessons in the High Magickal Arts, by Donald Michael Kraig (Llewellyn Publications, 1988)

The Light of Sex: Initiation, Magic, and Sacrament,
by Maria de Naglowska (author), Donald Traxler (translator, Introduction), and Hans Thomas Hakl (Foreword) (Inner Traditions, April 11, 2011)

Tantra and Sex

The Six Yogas of Naropa: Tsongkhapa's Commentary Entitled "A Book of Three Inspirations: A Treatise on the Stages of Training in the Profound Path of Naro's Six Dharmas," by Tsong-Kha-Pa (author), and Glenn C. Mullin (translator) (Snow Lion, October 4, 2005)

The Practice of the Six Yogas of Naropa, by Glenn C. Mullin (editor), and Glenn H. Mullin (translator) (Snow Lion, July 10, 2006)

Selected Works of the Dalai Lama II: The Tantric Yogas of Sister Niguma, by Dalai Lama II Dge-Dun-Rgya-Mtsho, Glenn Mullin, and Zasep Rinpoche (Snow Lion, May 1985)

The Bliss of Inner Fire: Heart Practice of the Six Yogas of Naropa, by Lama Thubten Yeshe (author), Robina Courtin (editor), Ailsa Cameron (editor), Jonathan Landaw (Introduction), and Lama Thubten Zopa Rinpoche (Foreword) (Wisdom Publications, June 1, 1998)

Kiss of the Yogini: "Tantric Sex" in its South Asian Contexts, by David Gordon White (University of Chicago Press, August 15, 2006)

The Alchemical Body: Siddha Traditions in Medieval India, by David Gordon White (University of Chicago Press, December 1, 1998)

Lust for Enlightenment: Buddhism and Sex, by John Stevens (Shambhala, December 8, 1990)

Taoist Sexual Alchemy

Taoist Secrets of Love: Cultivating Male Sexual Energy, by Mantak Chia (author) and Michael Winn (collaborator) (Aurora Press, June 1984)

The Multi-Orgasmic Man: Sexual Secrets Every Man Should Know, by Mantak Chia and Douglas Abrams (HarperCollins, February 23, 2010)

The Multi-Orgasmic Woman: Sexual Secrets Every Woman Should Know (Plus), by Mantak Chia and Rachel Carlton Abrams (HarperOne, February 23, 2010)

Taoist Yoga: Alchemy & Immortality, by Charles Luk and Lu K'uan Yu (Red Wheel/Weiser, January 1, 1999)

LGBTQIA Sexuality and Magic

Gay Witchcraft: Empowering the Tribe, by Christopher Penczak (Red Wheel/Weiser, June 1, 2003)

The Faggots and Their Friends Between Revolutions, by Larry Mitchell and Ned Asta (Calamus Books, May 1991)

Witchcraft and the Gay Counterculture, by Arthur Evans (Fag Rag Books, June 1978)

Index

A

abstinence, 73-76
acts of purification, 30-34
aetherial/etheric body, 25
AIDS, 24-25
Anahata Chakra, 44
anatomy, etheric body, 37-38
Angel Lover, Vision of the, 192-194
angels, 151-167
   being touched by, 164-167
anointing, the Elixir of Life and, 131
archangels, 157
artificial spirits, 137-149

astral body, location of the, 36
Astral Procreation, 138-139

B

basic breath meditation, 66-69
BDSM, 169-182
Bellows Breath, 64
belt channel, 40
binding, 174
Bindus, 49
body paints, sex sigil magic
   and, 113-115
body,
   aetherial/etheric, 25
   dangers of the, 29

empyrian/astral, 25
  material, 25, 36
  visualizations of the, 60-61
Bondage and Discipline,
  Dominance and Submission,
  Sadism and Masochism, see
  BDSM
bondage and edging, 175
Bounty of Zeus and Demeter,
  190-192
Branch Davidians, 26
breath
  play, 177-178
  purification, 31-32
  work, dangers of, 29
breath, importance of the, 54
breathing techniques, 53-69
breathing, nostril, 32
Buddha,
  teachings of the, 16-18
  transformation into the
    Guhyasamāja and, 16
Buddhists, purification and, 30
  celibacy, 25-26, 73-76
  sorcery of, 71-84

C

centers, 35-51
  energy-cycling experiment
    and, 112-113
  power, 42-43
central channel, the, 39
chakras, 42-43

changelings, fairies and, 160-161
channels, 35-51
Chaos Magic, 77
coercion, the sexual act and, 14
communication, sex and, 151
conjuration, sex and, 151
consent, the importance of, 14
control, artificial spirits and, 140
core center, 44
creating artificial spirits, rea
  sons for creating, 140-141
creation of life, 137
creative impulse, artificial
  spirits and, 141
Crowley, Aleister, 18, 116, 123,
  124-125, 144
crown center, 45
crystals, 156
cults, sex in smaller, 26
cycling energy, 110-112
cyclying through different
  centers, 112-113

D

dangers of sex, 29
Deity, highest sense of, 152
demonic possession, 23
demons, 151-167
deprivation, sensory, 173-175
divination, sex magic and,
  115-116

dominance roles, 171

drops, 35-51
  visualizing, 61

E

earth center, 46

edging and bondage, 175

ego, the orgasm and the, 100

ego-clinging, 28

elf sex, 160-161

Elixir of Life creation, Inner Heat and the, 125-127

Elixir of Life, 119-135
  artificial spirits and, 143

Embryonic Breath, 65-66

empyrian/astral body, 25

energetic body, dangers of the, 29

energy,
  celibacy and, 74
  cycling, 110-112

energy-cycling experiment, 112-113

enlightenment, sensory pleasure and, 15

eroto-comatose lucidity, 115-117

etheric body anatomy, 37-38

etheric body, location of the, 36

evocation of spirits, sex for, 154-157

expectations, fulfilling gender, 13

experimenting with your sexual orientation, 27

expiration dates for artificial spirits, 143

exploring your partner, 106-108

F

Faerie sex, 160-161

Faeries, 160

feet centers, 49

female menses, 122-123

fire, visualization of the, 62-63

five sheaths of Hinduism, 36

five stages of orgasm, 101

flagellation, striking and, 176

fluid retention during orgasm, 102-104

fluid retention, 82-84

fluids, men releasing their sexual, 13

foreplay, body paint and, 113-114

4 Rites of Sexual Sorcery, 183-195

front channel points, 48

front channel, 40-41

G

Gahndhi, celibacy and, 73

gender orientation, 12-14

gender roles, 171

goddesses, importance of, 86-104

gods and mortals, the pairing of, 178

gods,
  importance of, 86-104
  LGBT, 88-89
  nontraditional pairings for, 89-91

sex with, 151-167
traditional pairings of, 88
G-spot, your angle and hitting the, 126
Guhyasamāja Tantra, 15, 17
Buddha transforming into the, 16
Guru Yoga prayers, 17

H

hand centers, 48
heart center, 44
Heaven's Gate, 26
Higher Method, the, 96-97
Hinduism, five sheaths of, 36
HIV, 24-25
homosexual sex magic, 13
homosexuality, society and, 24
Homunculi, 137-149
the creation of, 144
HPV, 24-25
human sacrifice, 180-182

I

Incubus, 157, 160
innate divinity, unlocking, 13
Inner Fire
and sex, 108-110
meditation, 108
practice, masturbation and the, 81
technique, orgasms and the, 83
techniques, 53-69

Inner Fire,
dangers of, 63-64
effects of, 63-64
overview of the, 60
the Third Eye and, 115
Inner Heat and Elixir creation, 125-127
Inner heat technique, 13
Inner Heat, sexual energy and, 108
inner purification, 30-31
invoke, how to, 92-97

K

Khabbalah, four main bodies of, 36
King Indrabhuti, 16-18
kink, society and, 24

L

left channel, 39-40
LGBT gods, 88-89
life, the creation of, 137
limb channel, 41
lucid dream state, techniques for obtaining the, 159-160

M

Manipura Chakra, 45
masturbation,
society and, 24
sorcery of, 71-84
the benefits of, 76
material body, 25, 36
meditation,
basic breath, 66-69

Inner Fire and, 108
  white star purification, 32
men and multiple orgasms, 13
men and releasing sexual fluids, 13
menses, female, 122-123
mental body, dangers of the, 29
middle lock, Vase Breath and
  the, 58-59
monotheistic pairing, 91-92
moral decay, 23
morality and sex, 24
mortals and gods, the pairing
  of, 178
Muladhara Chakra, 45
multi-orgasms, male, 82-83
multiple orgasms, men and, 13

N

nocturnal emissions, 157
nontraditional pairings for
  gods, 89-91
nostril breathing, 32
nuance, artificial spirits and, 140
Nyams, meditation and, 69

O

objections, dealing with, 11
offerings to spirits, 151
oral consumption of the Elixir
  of Life, 130-131
oral sex, mutual, 131
oral stimulation, cycling and, 113

Ordo Templi Orientis, the, 26
orgasm and the ego, 100
orgasm,
  energy of the, 54
  five stages of, 101
  fluid retention during, 102-104
  quality of the, 80-81
  simultaneous, 102
  stopping your, 103
  strategic, 100-102
  the difference between men
    and women's, 13
  timeframe for a female, 101
orientation,
  gender, 12-14
  sexual, 12-14
outer purification, 30-31

P

passion,
  sense of being divine and, 98
  the definition of, 28
  the perils of, 23-34
patriarchy, 12-13
penis, withdrawing the Elixir of
  Life with the, 127-130
performing menial tasks,
  artificial spirits and, 141
philosophy of sexual magic, 21
physical dangers of sex, 29
Poliphilo, the story of, 19-21
polyamory, society and, 24
Popobawa, 157
positions, sexual, 99

power centers, 42-43

prayers, Guru Yoga, 17

pregnancy, 24-25

primal power, sex and, 26

psychogones, 139-140

psychological health, BDSM and, 171

Pulsing the Web, 106

purification meditation, white star, 32

purification, acts of, 30-34

R

Raeliens, 26

Rajneesh, 26

rear channel points, 47-48

rear channel, 40-41

red drops, 62, 122-123

Reverse Breath, 64-65

right channel, 39-40

Rite of Harmonia, 184-188

rituals, correct practice for, 195

root center, 45

root lock, Vase Breath and the, 57

S

sacrifice, human, 180-182

safe words, 172-173

Sahasrara Chakra, 45

Sai Baba Movement, the, 26

scouraging, 175-177

scrying mirrors, 156
  Elixir of Life and, 134-135

scrying, 173-175

secret purification, 30-31

seed, cultivating, 121

semen, magic used with, 120-121

sensory
  deprivation, 173-175
  pleasure and enlightenment, 15

sex for evocation of spirits, 154-157

sex magic and divination, 115-116

sex sigil magic, 113-115

sexual activity, focusing on magic during, 80

sexual energy,
  circulation of, 111
  Inner Heat and, 108

sexual fluid, female, 122

sexual fluids, the sorcery of, 119

sexual magic, philosophy behind, 21

sexual orientation, 12-14
  experimenting outside of your, 27

sexual sorcery, the dangers of, 23-34

sexual stimulation, awakening through, 117

sexuality, controlling, 73

Siddha Asanga, 15

sigil
  creation, 77
  spell, 77-81

sigils, artificial spirits and, 141-142

Simple Sigil of Mercury, 188-189

simultaneous orgasm, 102

skull, sex with a, 146-149

sleep paralysis, 157

solar essence, your partner's, 111-112

solar plexus center, 45

spectrophilia, 157

sperm,
    cultivating, 121
    incubating the, 121

spirit communication, sex and, 151

spirits,
    artificial, 137-149
    offerings to, 15
    sex for evocation of, 154-157
    sex with, 151-167

spiritual stories, the importance of, 15

star center, 46

STDs, 24-25

stimuli, supernormal, 71-72

strategic orgasm, 100-102

striking and flagellation, 176

submission, forcing people into, 25

submissive role, 171

Succubus, 157, 158, 160

supernatural powers, Homunculi, 144

supernormal stimuli, 71-72

T

talismans,
    anointing of, 133-135
    Elixir of Life and, 124

tantra, practicing, 27

Taoism, techniques drawn from, 11

temples, power centers at the, 47

The Family International, 26

Third Eye, 46-47
    sending energy to the, 116
    the genitals and the, 113
    the Inner Fire and the, 115
    the Thunderbolt Technique and the, 128
    Vase Breath and the, 56

throat center, 46

Thunderbolt Technique, 128

tradition, an overview of, 38

traditional pairings of gods, 88

Trauco of Chile, 157

Trul Khors exercises, 108

U

uniting, 97-98

Universal Centering Rite, 97

upper lock, Vase Breath and the, 57-58

V

Vajroli Mudra, 119-120
    sex abuse scandals and the, 129
    withdrawing fluid and the, 127-129

variations, an overview of, 38

Vase Breath, 55-56
   all locks and the, 59-60
   locks applying locks to the, 56
   middle lock and the, 58-59
   performing locks and the, 61
   root lock and the, 57
   upper lock and the, 57-58
   creating the Elixir of Life
     and, 125

Vulcanic Base Breaths, 125

W

whipping, 175-177

white drops, 62
   the, 120-121

white star purification
   meditation, 32

withdrawing fluid, the penis
   and, 127

words, safe, 172-173

About the Author

When he was just 5 years old, Jason Miller (Inominandum) had a series of psychic experiences that sparked his interest in the occult. He took up the practice of both High Magick and Hoodoo Rootworking while still a teenager, learning how ceremonial and folk magic can work together and complement each other.

He has been involved with a number of orders and groups over the years, always seeking the quintessence of the arte. He has traveled to New Orleans to study Hoodoo, Europe to study witchcraft and ceremonial magick, and Nepal to study tantra. Miller is an initiated Tantrika in the Nyingma and Bon lineages of Tibet, an ordained Gnostic Bishop, and a member of the Chthonic Ouranian Temple and the Sangreal Sodality.

He is the author of:

Protection & Reversal Magick: A Witch's Defense Manual

The Sorcer's Secrets: Strategies in Practical Magic

Financial Sorcery: Magical Strategies to Create Real and Lasting Wealth

The Strategic Sorcery course

The Strategic Sorcery blog

Miller lives with his wife on the New Jersey shore, where he practices and teaches magick professionally. Visit him at *www.strategicsorcery.net*.

ABOUT THE ILLUSTRATOR

Mathew Brownlee is an occultist, kung fu master, and tattoo artist located in Philadelphia, Pennsylvania. He is a member of the Chthonic Auranian Temple, and is a Tantrika in the Nyingma and Bon lineages of Tibet. He is a graduate of the Philadelphia Art Institute and works at Baker Street Tattoo in Media, Pennsylvania. Visit him at *www.bakerstreettattoo.com*.